Actress and author of the courageous *New York Times* bestselling memoir *High on Arrival*, Mackenzie Phillips brings her knowledge and voice to the subject of recovery for the first time.

As the daughter of the founder of the 1960s band The Mamas and the Papas, Mackenzie grew up in a dysfunctional environment and subsequently battled a near-fatal drug addiction. Now a drug and alcohol counselor and outspoken advocate for addiction awareness and education, she gets real about the hard times of recovery, how to get through them, and the joy of experiencing life clean and sober.

Used by both recovering addicts and their families, Mackenzie's book is a message of hope and a reminder that sobriety is a lifelong journey of the spirit that allows us to lift ourselves up even when we stumble and fall.

More Praise for Mackenzie Phillips's

Hopeful Healing

"This book will lovingly hold your hand through anything you need to know about recovery and addiction, or really, just getting through life. This is the Mackenzie I know: smart, funny, warm—she has that great 'been there, done that' attitude and just tells it like it is, without judgment. Read this book now. It's your soft place to fall."
—**Valerie Bertinelli**, actress and *New York Times* bestselling author

"This wonderful book offers a powerful and unique perspective of the recovery process. Its conversational style pulls us deep into the 'heart of our own heart,' and helps us view the challenges of our lives through the lens of Mackenzie's life experience. The truth is we are all on the path of healing, and these essays help us view our own lives with hopeful reverence."
—**James Twyman**, *New York Times* bestselling author

"*Hopeful Healing* is a riveting and well-documented account of the messy yet beautiful experience of recovering from addiction. Through a series of intimate and illuminating conversations, Mackenzie Phillips leaves no stone unturned, exploring topics that range from shame and guilt to forgiveness, hope, fear, grace, and more. Indeed, we do recover, and Mackenzie Phillips is as fine an example of that as I've ever seen."
—**Chris Grosso**, author of *Indie Spiritualist* and *Everything Mind*

"A light is a light is a light. And Mack, as her friends call her, has shone at every stage: the winsome child, the actress-to-be, the churlish star, and even the anodyne who got lost and clawed her way back from the surface of Mars with a wisdom that mines the core stuff of life—or hope—as the key that unlocks anyone's near-impenetrable fortress of addiction.

But see? Little Laura has done it!

And it's shared here with every word of *Hopeful Healing*."

—**Billy Corgan**, cofounder of the Smashing Pumpkins, poet, contrarian

Hopeful Healing

Hopeful Healing

Essays on Managing Recovery
and Surviving Addiction

Mackenzie Phillips

ATRIA PAPERBACK
New York London Toronto Sydney New Delhi

BEYOND WORDS
Hillsboro, Oregon

ATRIA PAPERBACK
An Imprint of Simon & Schuster, Inc.
1230 Avenue of the Americas
New York, NY 10020

BEYOND WORDS
20827 N.W. Cornell Road, Suite 500
Hillsboro, Oregon 97124-9808
503-531-8700 / 503-531-8773 fax
www.beyondword.com

This publication contains the opinions and ideas of its author. It is intended to provide helpful and informative material on the subjects addressed in the publication. It is sold with the understanding that the author and publisher are not engaged in rendering medical, health, or any other kind of personal professional services in the book. The reader should consult his or her medical, health, or other competent professional before adopting any of the suggestions in this book or drawing inferences from it. The author and publisher specifically disclaim all responsibility for any liability, loss, or risk, personal or otherwise, which is incurred as a consequence, directly or indirectly, of the use and application of any of the contents of this book.

Managing editor: Lindsay S. Easterbrooks-Brown
Editors: Anna Noak, Nevin Mays, Emmalisa Sparrow Wood
Copyeditor: Vinnie Kinsella
Proofreader: Jennifer Weaver-Neist
Cover design: Devon Smith
Composition: William H. Brunson Typography Services

First Atria Paperback/Beyond Words trade paperback edition February 2017

For more information about special discounts for bulk purchases, please contact Simon & Schuster Special Sales at 1-866-506-1949 or business@simonandschuster.com.

The Simon & Schuster Speakers Bureau can bring authors to your live event. For more information or to book an event, contact the Simon & Schuster Speakers Bureau at 1-866-248-3049 or visit our website at www.simonspeakers.com.

Manufactured in the United States of America

10 9 8 7 6 5 4 3 2 1

Library of Congress Cataloging-in-Publication Data

Names: Phillips, Mackenzie, author.
    Title: Hopeful healing : essays on managing recovery and surviving addiction
/ Mackenzie Phillips.
        Description: New York ; Hillsboro, Oregon : Atria Paperback/Beyond Words, [2017] |
    Includes bibliographical references.
    Identifiers: LCCN 2016041064 (print) | LCCN 2016056854 (ebook) |
        ISBN 9781582705705 (pbk.) | ISBN 9781501110573 (eBook)
    Subjects: LCSH: Addicts--Rehabilitation. | Alcoholics--Rehabilitation. |
        Substance abuse--Treatment. | Phillips, Mackenzie.
    Classification: LCC HV4998 .P495 2017 (print) | LCC HV4998 (ebook) |
        DDC 616.86/03--dc23
    LC record available at https://lccn.loc.gov/2016041064

The corporate mission of Beyond Words Publishing, Inc.: *Inspire to Integrity*

I would like to dedicate this book to my mother,
Suzy Phillips January
May 27, 1936–June 18, 2016

"I'll love you forever,
I'll like you for always,
As long as I'm living
my mommy you'll be."
—From *Love You Forever*
by Robert N. Munsch

And to all creatures great and small,
most especially to Shane

And to Freddie the Noble Pug
July 17, 2000–July 4, 2014
RIP

Hope begins in the dark, the stubborn hope that if you just show up and try to do the right thing, the dawn will come.
You wait and watch and work: you don't give up.

—**Anne Lamott**

CONTENTS

Foreword

by Brad Lamm

Tiny, we were. Remember? Think back. As far as you can muster. As kids, remember just how little we were, with more energy than our bodies could contain at times. We were growing, so the engine revved and moved and kept us going like there was a supersized battery inside of us. We were passengers on this zany adventure.

I remember how I ran and soared from dawn till dusk with, sometimes, just the mosquitos keeping me company in Eugene, Oregon. Never enough hours in the day!

As a man, I roamed from continent to countryside, wandering in my child's mind; sparked in spirit by the books I had as constant companions. With an always-moving mind and feet to match, I was drifting and dreaming of the next adventure; a dirty, scuffed-up big kid with books in my bag to keep me company.

When I met Mack the first time, I connected with her energy and wandering spirit. Mack has traveled down streets and through spots that we've seen, some on TV and screen, but mostly, as I've come to know and value her, it's her inside journey that moves me.

If we are all born as passengers on a trip, then how good might we get? I asked Mack that very question one day, after we'd known each other for bit. We were at the Pacific Ocean, walking on the sand, feet in and out of the chilly sea. She considered the question and smiled.

Far from the Mack that made *TMZ* buzz that day, all those years ago, for getting busted at LAX for drug possession, this Mack considered and smiled and paused, and I got how I was to be part of her journey. I knew that, not that day but soon, I would get to witness her moving from student to teacher in this grand third act of hers.

We work together. Mack comes to work before everyone else. First in. Last out. She's like a first responder running into the building to support and steady those trying to get through the trauma-informed recovery program I founded, and where she is a passenger now, too, with me. It's called Breathe Life Healing Center, and I get to witness how good she is getting.

I once asked Mackenzie, "When you were a little girl, what did you want to be when you grew up?"

"I wanted to be a fireman. Or a nun," she told me. Her mom's response to the dream went like this: "Only boys can be firemen. Nuns have to marry Jesus, so you couldn't have a boyfriend."

"So I decided I wanted to be an abnormal psychiatrist, so I could understand why people do what they do." Mack told me she had decided this by ten. As we all know, by twelve, she'd ditched psychiatry for the big silver screen, and America not only got a sweetheart to grow up with but she found a new set of dreams to guide her. Finally, she's come back around to help others remember who they are.

As a boy, I swam in childlike wonder peppering myself with questions, wondering, *What does this mean?* and *What might this do?* and *What might I do one day?* and even *How good might I get?*

I was constantly wondering, *How good might I get?* Not "good" like "momma's good boy" but good in terms of a useful mind, and a curious spirit, and feet to take me great places. Imagine this notion as you consider that curious little Mackenzie. The Mackenzie I fell in step with for the very first time on TV as a kid, the second time when she appeared on screen in *American Graffiti*.

In my mind, Mackenzie was a kindred spirit from a different time, grabbing for her slice of adventure. Later, as Julie Cooper popped up on *One Day at a Time*, I found a wise-cracking and curious sidekick to play with once a week, no matter what.

Then things changed. Mackenzie was the first peer I remember seeing struggle with drugs. I wondered where my adventurous friend had gone and soon discovered exactly where she'd checked into, as I landed there too. Turns out we'd both gone down a rabbit hole of adventures, dangerous and terrifying at times.

We got better—we did—and now we thrive. Our very states of being have changed. We went from longing to die and end this thing to swimming in a beautiful journey, and recovering love and family and truth and joy along the way.

I love hearing Mack's stories, and I know *Hopeful Healing* will take you where it's taken me—to laughter and reconsidering what I dreamed of as a boy. She took me on a trip for two of remembering the life we've had, the jobs we've spun, the loves we've encountered.

Mack reminds me every day to b-r-e-a-t-h-e. As living, breathing human beings, we are wired to breathe and dream. To dream, discover, and wonder as passengers on this delicious journey.

Brad Lamm, author, teacher, and interventionist,
and the founder of Breathe Life Healing Centers.

Foreword

by Glenn Scarpelli

Laura Mackenzie Phillips has been my friend and spiritually adopted sister since I was fourteen years old. I think about the many chapters we've shared over the years. We've experienced births, deaths, celebrations, tears, successes, and disappointments. I've seen Mack at her best and at her worst. I've watched my friend transform, grow, collapse, and rise again. I knew her dad and I know her son. I've seen the joys and heartaches that relationships have brought. Basically, what I'm saying is, I've seen the real person. A real person with real-life circumstances, like any of us.

Mack has been in the public eye since she was a kid, and I feel sometimes people have preconceived notions of who she is. But let me tell you . . . she is funny, happy, talented, smart, and incredibly generous—always has been. She can also be vulnerable, shy at times, insecure, and incredibly sensitive. Like I said, a real person like any of us. Life is multifaceted, and she has been one of my teachers in learning how to accept and embrace it *all*.

She and I don't look back and say "the good ol' days" because we know the best of times is *now*. I'm so proud of the person she is today! I've literally watched her come face to face with her pain, fear, and that empty void in her heart. Now she has filled that void with self-love and peace of mind.

As you read this book, you will see how she has taken her life experience and turned it into solid wisdom that she is determined to share, strictly to help others. This taps into her life's purpose. Her message is authentic. For me, she is an example of transformation and evolution, a role model of strength and overcoming, but most of all, she is my friend . . . And for that, I am most grateful.

Glenn Scarpelli, former One Day at a Time *costar*
and owner of Sedona NOW TV

Hope is being able to see that there is light despite all of the darkness.

—Desmond Tutu

Preface

This book is the result of a series of long conversations that occurred over the course of several months. I'd decided I wanted to create something that expressed my passion for educating and helping people affected by addiction. I also wanted to speak to the thousands upon thousands of people who have sent me messages saying that my memoir, *High on Arrival*, helped them find their truth. They inspire me every day to continue to speak my own truth and to continue to share my story.

As I gave different television and radio interviews over time, I realized that I had a solid base of information to share with those impacted by addiction and with those who wanted to pursue recovery. So I sat down with a collaborator and we talked. We talked about all of the things that people struggle with as they start the process and of all the misunderstood aspects of addiction. We talked about it through the lens of my own experiences and what I have learned and observed of others' experiences. From there, we compiled these little essays on different aspects of recovery.

In these essays, I've concentrated on the concepts and feelings that surround the recovery process rather than on the linear story of my life and recovery. I wanted to preserve the conversational foundation of these essays so that they would provide a genuine experience, and hopefully, the person reading them would find a friend and some words that are helpful along their own journey.

This is a wisdom-based book, not a clinical book. This is also a conversational book. While I do include some basic facts about substance use disorders, I make no claim to being an expert on all things addiction and recovery. I am, however, an expert in my own experiences of those two things, and it is in this that I have found the strongest connection with my clients at the recovery center where I work.

My own recovery began in the 12-step tradition, first introduced in the early twentieth century. The language and the culture from that tradition permeate the language of addiction and recovery in general, and it is also woven throughout this book. Over time, as I continued my journey and learned more about my substance use disorder, I began integrating other methods into my own recovery strategy. This book is an amalgam of all of these things mixed in with a huge dose of my own experiences.

Before you dive in, I want to say thank you for being brave enough to work toward recovery, to learn about recovery, or whatever else might have you picking up *Hopeful Healing*. I wrote this for you.

Hope Is the Thing

On what this book is about and how to use it

*Hope is the thing with feathers that perches in the soul
and sings the tune without the words
and never stops at all.*

—Emily Dickinson

This is a book about addiction and hope.

These are not two things normally associated with one another, but oddly enough, when you think about addiction and hope, they have the same kind of dynamic. Addiction does not discriminate, and neither does hope. The disease of addiction doesn't differentiate between age, race, location, or socioeconomic status. Neither does hope.

Addiction can do what it does because it's an opportunistic, physiological illness, meaning the potential for being an addict already lives biologically in some of us—mostly due to the wiring in our brains. All it takes to kick it off is the introduction of the drug of choice. Then the drug becomes something else: an entity residing inside you.

Hope can do what it does because it, too, is opportunistic and it, too, lives inside us. But here is where hope shifts gears: it does not need outside encouragement to activate it. It is an embedded impulse that naturally resides within. At its core, hope comes from a belief that there is potential for something better, no matter the odds. And it takes only a moment of experiencing that belief to trigger hope.

Maybe I should say that this book is about recognizing that moment. In that moment lives hope. Hope is what fuels recovery, and recovery is what saves an addict's life—your life, whether you are an active addict or have just started recovery or have relapsed. Wherever you are on your journey, this book is for you.

I am an addict. It is hope and living my recovery that save my life every day.

One of the biggest issues with treating addiction is that, when substance use is involved, it's hard to remember that there is a fully realized self living under the disease.

So I want to put this out there for everyone right up front:

Dear Reader,

Hi, my name is Laura Mackenzie Phillips, and I'm a real person with a real life. I'm also a mom, a daughter, a sister, and a friend. I'm a counselor, a seeker, a caregiver, and an advocate for what I believe in.

P.S. I live with and manage a disease called addiction.

That sounds so easy, but the reality is that it takes a long time to go from writing a letter about yourself in which addiction is the only topic to making addiction a postscript in a letter that is full of the life that happens when you live sober.

In my active addiction, my letter went primarily like this:

[No greeting]
Heroin. Alcohol. Pills. Cocaine.
[No closing]

In recovery, my letter is still being written, and it will be the longest letter ever if I keep writing. It starts with a greeting—*Hello, my darling!* And I know it will end with love—*All my love, Mack.* The ups and downs of my everyday life are filling the pages between.

Hope has become a thematic part of my letter. I share my experience of it and with it because of the lessons and wisdom I have gained from it. I believe that hope, the lessons hope teaches, and the wisdom hope brings are things meant to be shared with others. Even if these messages are only shared with one other person, these things are worth passing on.

So let's begin, shall we?

In these pages, I will share my experiences with addiction and recovery, and I hope that what I have learned and the hard-won wisdom I have gained serve you well.

Why This Book

My journey of recovery has been a public one—ugh! I'm a celebrity; and while I hope that people primarily know me for my advocacy, the reality is I'm probably most associated with my acting in movies like *American Graffiti* and on the TV show *One Day at a Time*, my experiences with *Celebrity Rehab*, and the controversy surrounding my memoir, *High on Arrival*. This level of visibility within the public eye has been both good and bad. My ups have been seen and enjoyed by many. My downs have also been public, often humiliating, always heartrending, and unfortunately, enjoyed by some. My relationships with my family members have been detailed and judged by the media right alongside my addiction.

Having strangers make judgments and give uninformed commentary on your life is a hugely disempowering and depressing experience; it steals your voice from your own story. That's one side of the coin. The other side is that my celebrity status has given me a platform to speak as an advocate for substance-use education and awareness, both of which are more important than ever before.

Why? Because it's happening in our national backyard. Even though the future's looking brighter (for example, President Obama proposed $1.1 billion in new funding for the 2017 fiscal year to address the prescription-opioid-abuse and heroin-use epidemic), the statistics are still grim.[1] In a study published in 2014, there were 127,000 deaths caused by drug disorders in 2013 in the United States alone (up from 53,000 in 1990).[2] Furthermore, there is a large treatment gap between those who need help and those who get help. In 2013, around 23 million Americans needed treatment for a substance disorder but only around 2.5 million ended up receiving care and treatment.[3] In 2014 alone, of the 16.3 million adults and 679,000 adolescents who had an AUD (alcohol use disorder), less than 10 percent of both age groups were actually treated. Specifically, 1.5 million adults received treatment, which only addressed 9.8 percent of the men and 7.4 percent of the women who needed help. For adolescents, the need addressed was around 8 percent, or 55,000 (18,000 males and 37,000 females).[4] (Keep in mind that, although the substances may differ, alcohol and drug addiction are both from the same substance use disorder.)

These are statistics you can find with any basic research on addiction. What these statistics don't tell you is what it means to be a person who has this disease; the numbers don't tell you that the addict lives in a state of hopelessness.

This hopelessness is revealed in your daily reality if you have an addictive disorder. The stakes are as personal as they are high—so high that the truth is many of us die. We die before we can get sober. We die because we're driving intoxicated. We die because we're stealing something from somebody. We die because we think we can handle the next shot, and then it's over. Boom. The stakes are high because we break the hearts of everyone around us. They're high because we have no relationship with ourselves. With realities like this to face, no wonder addicts live in a state of perpetual hopelessness.

But there is hope despite these high stakes. The situation is so dire that the world is slowly changing its behavior in order to face addiction. I want to be on the forefront of this change. I want to be on the front line of this uniting movement to face addiction, because it is one of the biggest health crises this country has ever seen. People are beginning to wake up to see the toll addiction is taking on our brothers, our sisters, our children, our parents, and ourselves.

If ever there was a time to get on the recovery train, this is it. For yourself, for your loved ones, and for your fellow addicts. The growing awareness that is emerging all around us is its own kind of support. People want you to get help—they're not just trying to kill your buzz. They want you to be well, they want you to live, and they have hope for you. Take it.

My Heart As the Author

Before you delve into the book, I want to talk about how I will relate to you as an author.

Although I work as a counselor at a treatment center, I don't have very many years of experience on that side of the desk. What I do have is the intuitive understanding that comes from a level of firsthand knowledge and the wisdom gained from my own perspective. Life experience informs a lot of what I do when working with a client and, thus, also informs the content of this book.

I'm at my best when I'm showing up with all of my knowledge and wisdom to work with clients, using clinical interventions presented in ways addicts can hear. I don't have all the answers, but what I do have is an amazing clinical supervisor, my personal experience with substance abuse, and—sometimes most important—the ability to know when I don't have all of the answers.

My intention as author is to show you, the reader, through my own story and my own experiences, that it's possible to leave the hopelessness of addiction behind and rediscover who you really are. I've done that climb more than once, and I know how it goes. It can be overwhelming and terrifying.

We're all perpetual students of life. The good and the bad situations have things to teach us. Sometimes we gain wisdom, and sometimes we ignore the wisdom that's offered. I've taken extended courses on how to be an addict, and I've also taken a ton on how to be in recovery. I've learned that fellowship of some kind is essential; I've learned that when my addiction is active, I'm lost in it. Recovery is about rising out of that abyss and, for me, hopefully helping others do the same.

I've never recovered alone—I've tried, and it's never worked. There have always been people around me to help me through—this is important. Addiction is isolation, loneliness, and chaos. You can be surrounded by a bunch of other users going through similar experiences, but when it comes down to it, you're still alone with your drug—the only two in the room.

There is a reason why sitting around in a church basement or community center is such an intrinsic part of recovery. Witnessing someone else's journey lets us see ourselves in different packaging. This allows us see to our own disconnection and our own potential. Hearing someone else's story that is similar to our own allows us to experience empathy, truth, and ultimately, hope—and hope is the amazing engine that drives recovery.

This process is also about self-care and self-compassion. Empathy for yourself is just as important as empathy for others. It's not just about putting down the drugs; it's about learning how to care for yourself in a mindful way—like you would a dear friend.

When I have living examples of others who have been in my shoes, my journey isn't so isolated and dark; there are guides and lights that help me on my way. I hope to be one of those guides for you. It can be a scary and difficult road to walk, but it's also one that's always easier to walk together.

Throughout this book, I offer you what I have learned as someone with a substance use disorder and as a counselor. I tell my personal truths and share my clinical understanding of this disease. I offer up tools that have worked for me, and I talk about the methods of treatment that are broadly accepted and used in the recovery process.

What I don't offer are definitive answers. Every person's path to recovery is different; therefore, everyone's course of treatment—be it through a residential program, a 12-step program, or another treatment option—will be personal. My intention for you, as I share my story and perspectives, is that you find something you can use here to help you climb out of the rabbit hole of addiction—that this book offers understanding when you need it, compassion when it's hard to find, and a moment for you to find your hope engine.

How to Use This Book

Well, first, read it!

As I was working on this book, one of the things I had to figure out was what belonged in here and what didn't. I knew that I didn't want to do a step-by-step recovery book; there are a lot of those out there. What I really wanted to do, I realized, was to share information on what helped me make it through and I wanted to give it to you straight, because there isn't any other way to deal with addiction. And this meant acknowledging the everyday realities of recovery—that there are good days and there are bad days.

One of the things I think about a lot is the emotional life of an addict in early recovery. In early recovery, it's vital to understand that your behavior is the same as when you were using; it's just that the drug is missing. Since addiction is physiological in origin but manifests itself in behavior, when an addict begins the recovery process, they also begin the hard task of carving out a new way to survive without the drug, without the drink (from here on, I'm going to use *drugs* as a catchall term that includes alcohol). With this in mind, I've focused throughout the book on the emotions that start hitting us in the first stages of recovery. A huge part of how we maintain our recovery is based on how we learn to fully manage our emotions and thinking in a healthy way.

Obviously, you're going to have good days and bad days—and what I mean by that is absolutely fucking excellent days and really shitty days. The journey lies in how to manage both as they come, and how to blend the two types of days into an existence so positive that the idea of using or drinking isn't even on the table. Addicts do some messed up stuff when their addiction is active. I shot up cocaine while pregnant with my son. The horror of my actions in sober retrospect is something that I deal with to this day. During my recovery, I've felt a whole range of emotions—everything from fear to shame to horrible sadness. This is not just a me thing—the vast majority of addicts feel a range of emotions in recovery based on the choices we made and actions we took in our active addiction. This is the emotional landscape where many of our triggers reside, and so I decided to dedicate chapters of my book to covering such topics as fear and trust.

I wanted to also make sure I covered things like mindfulness and negative self-talk. Both are endemic concepts in recovery. I cover some basics like addiction and recovery terminology, stereotypes, and well-known methods for recovery. These are sprinkled throughout the chapters and are meant to help those new to recovery to understand what they are going through within the context of a variety of treatment pathways.

This book covers a range of topics that someone in recovery may encounter and perhaps struggle with. On the flip side, I have also included real-life stories and personal experiences that *show* you why recovery is the best decision you will ever make as a person with a substance use disorder; I'm not going to just tell you so and expect you to believe me. Trust is as important between us as it is on your own journey to recovery.

You can read this book in order or you can jump to whatever area of your recovery you're working on. I structured it this way because, as I've mentioned, everyone's addiction acts differently and recovery is an individual experience. This means that treatment and tools need to be adaptable to each person. So use the book in whatever way you like as you travel down your path. Use it as a tool, and know that when you begin to manage your addiction, you are in the very act of saving your own life; you are hope in action.

FINALLY

I opened this introduction with a quote from an Emily Dickinson poem. I chose this quote because I think that it speaks a deep truth about recovery—that recovery is possible because hope, no matter how extreme your situation may be, is a living thing that is always within you.

One of the central themes in this book and in recovery is the power of language. How we name, define, and contextualize ourselves matters. The stories we tell of who we are and how we got here matter. The ideas and burgeoning hopes we express for our future matter. Because of this, I recommend you start writing.

Your writing can be a journal or a daily note to yourself. It can be a list of all of your questions for the day or a list of everything you're grateful for. You can write letters to yourself—whatever works for you. Grab a journal, some stationery, a pad of paper, your notes app on your phone or iPad—again, whatever works. Just keep it handy. This is your place to pull out what's in your head and see it in black and white. It's your place to say "Ah-ha!" or "I'm calling bullshit!" as you make discoveries about yourself, your disorder, and what recovery holds for you.

IT WORKS IF YOU WORK IT

Write a letter of introduction about yourself in which your addiction is just the postscript (see my example on page xxvi). It can be a letter expressing who you are now or who you wish to be. Let me help you get started:

Dear World,
I am a . . .

Hopeful Healing

Road Trips

On defining addiction and finding

its place in your story

If we are facing in the right direction,
all we have to do is keep on walking.

—Zen proverb

One of the most powerful things you can do for yourself is to dive deep into understanding your addiction, to clearly and honestly tell your story for yourself—all of your history and your behavior within that history, and what role your addiction played in it.

Like any trip, every addiction has a beginning. It's marked on the map that recovering addicts keep within their mind—the map that they pull out and examine when they need to remind themselves of the road they've traveled and the road they want to be on as they move forward.

Your addiction may have started long before you found your drug of choice. Russell Brand has a great story in his book *My Booky Wook: A Memoir of Sex, Drugs, and Stand-Up* about eating tons of chocolate when he was a boy as a way to compensate for feeling "tubby and useless" around his father. "Tubby because I sought solace in chocolate consumption, the foil wrappers of the delicious P-P-P-Penguin bars I'd scoff, a perspicacious trailer for the tinfoil tapestry I would later weave with smack and crack. I was a connoisseur of Penguin, which came in green, blue, and red wrappers. I was a particular devotee of the blue variety, even though all of the Penguins are the same below the surface . . ." Reflecting upon this childhood behavior gave him insight into the substance use disorder he struggled with as an adult.[1]

The truth for everyone with a substance use disorder is that you don't know *in the moment* that you've just marked the beginning of your addiction. It's something that can only be marked when we take a deep look at ourselves. Deep looks usually only happen when we're put into crisis. Until you take that look, it doesn't seem real.

My addiction rolled in over time and became my constant passenger and navigator. A really crappy navigator. Once my addiction was fully active, my life went to shit. It became a series of crises and a series of attempts at being clean, with episodes of deep denial in between. I tried rehab. A lot. Eleven fun-filled times. Those experiences could make up their own book if I rehashed them here (well, they already did: my last book). So to spare you and me both some time, here's a brief overview of my road trip as navigated by my not-so-trusty sidekick, addiction, whom I call Train Wreck.

One of the earlier times I went into rehab, it was my dad who decided I should go because "my life was a mess." (My dad's life was also a big mess at the time, and my going to rehab was a part of his going to rehab.) I had been fired from my job, my relationships were blowing up in my face, and I had overdosed and almost died, yet I absolutely did *not* think I had a problem. Train Wreck agreed—no problem whatsoever.

I did a six-week outpatient treatment program at a rehab center. I can tell you exactly what I didn't do there: I didn't do a deep self-evaluation, and I didn't take away any of the tools for recovery that were offered. I did, however, add a substance to my arsenal of stuff to feed the monster: alcohol. Oh, I'm sorry, did you want me to stay sober after rehab? *Seriously?*

Then I "recovered" and went on my merry way, having, by choice, learned next to nothing about my disease or myself. I white-knuckled it off of drugs but carried on with drinking and most of the addictive behaviors I'd entered rehab with. This was the time in my life when I would walk around going, "I'm clean," but avoid the word sober like the plague. I was clean but *not* sober—the difference between the two is kind of grey. Saying I was clean without the word sober felt like I was getting away with something. A fidgety-fudgety way of mincing words to escape detection.

I strongly suspect this was because I never really thought I had a problem. Sure, I had "problems," but they were bearable because of drugs and alcohol. My attitude was "don't even *try* to tell me I can't have my fix." It took me no time at all to start using again *and* to be fired again *and* to blow up my relationships again. After rehab,

I did do something new but not something positive: I entered a very dangerous drug scene and did several very dangerous drugs, both of which put me in seriously harmful situations physically and emotionally. But of course, I didn't have a problem. By this time, Train Wreck was behind the wheel and deciding where we would go. I had become a passenger in my life and didn't even know it.

The second significant time I tried to get clean, it was because I was pregnant and I realized my life was careening out of control. I was scared. *Really* scared. I abstained for less than a year before I started using again. Looking at it now, I realize that I had never truly stopped careening.

My life revolved around drugs. I had my son, Shane, but my center was drugs. He would be calling for me, knocking on the bathroom door, and I would be on the other side shooting up. In one of those moments, as Shane was calling out to me, I had this flash of clarity—a pivotal moment: I remembered being sixteen or seventeen and knocking on the bathroom door, looking for my dad, and hearing him say, "Not now, darling, Daddy's shooting up." I remembered it being so normal that it didn't even faze me.

Now, on Dad's side of the door, I realized I was re-creating history, except this time it was Shane outside the bathroom trying to get *my* attention.

Back when I was a teenager, I was so used to my dad shooting up that I knew I should just come back later, that the drugs came first. Did I want this to be Shane's experience ten, fifteen years from that moment? To be normalized to the closed door and being second place to my drug use?

It was this moment when I thought, *Oh my god, this is happening. Someone should do something about this.* And then I realized, *Wait, I'm that someone. I should do something about this.* In that moment, I woke the fuck up. I knew I had to break this cycle of addiction and neglect. I was the parent this time; my son was four. The person who was responsible and who had the power to take action was me.

Shane was on the other side of the door, and he needed me. I had never had someone need me before—someone who would be lost if I died from an overdose. I decided to go to rehab again to try to fix the world that I had created, so that Shane would grow up feeling safe and loved. I put down the needle, opened the bathroom door, and took responsibility for caring for my son and myself.

I checked into a place for those who are reluctant to recover. Really, I swear, that's part of their mission statement: "For the reluctant to recover."

It worked. I worked it.

I stayed sober for ten years. Train Wreck had moved to the back-seat and was taking a nice long nap.

Ten years sober. This was because I had started to really examine my life for the first time while I was in rehab, instead of just going through the motions. I began to learn about my disorder. I began to identify my patterns. I slowly created a sober self and began building a sober life. Those ten years contain some of my most beautiful and cherished memories, and are full of all of the collected moments of developing a meaningful relationship with my son.

So what happened? Well, outwardly I had it going on. My work, my family, my life—it was all very beautiful. But inwardly, I was still carrying a lot of emotional pain that was keeping Train Wreck in my backseat.

Life, being what it is, did not stay beautiful. It could have—*I* could have—but Train Wreck was growing restless in her sleep, and I didn't notice. Shit happened, as it does. Bumps and gaping potholes in the road. I chose to have elective surgery. I was in pain because my father was dying, and I wasn't working the program. The combo of deep emotional pain from my past and physical pain from my present was enough to re-engage my disease. I wasn't being self-aware, and I made choices that gave me access to drugs. Pain pills. Prescribed drugs. These are to an addict what bacon is to a reluctant vegetarian: one taste of either and you're right back where you started.

After sitting so quietly in the backseat for ten years, my passenger woke up and started to bark out direction, deciding the route again. I did try to take back control. I tried twice to detox again, but by then, Train Wreck had shoved her way from the backseat to the front; and her foot was covering mine and pushing down on the gas. And here's the kicker: Train Wreck was all me.

I called my old drug dealers (you know, to catch up). I then invited them to move in with me. Brilliant idea! No more having to leave the house to get more coke! What a load off. Pills *and* coke.

When the doctor caught on and the pills went away, I started using heroin—much like what's happening in the epidemic: as it gets harder to get legal pills, addicts make the jump to heroin. Believe me, it's happening to people you would never think it could happen to. This is one of the reasons we have to start adjusting our thinking about how addiction happens and who it happens to. When the pain in between shooting up the heroin got too bad and life became too real, I started using coke and heroin together. They call that speed-balling; I call it life destroying.

This period was and remains the darkest time in my life. I literally lived to shoot up, which is a god-awful way to live. It's speeding down the road at a thousand miles an hour without a seatbelt on. It's going through the windshield when you inevitably crash.

In the end, it was a trip to New York that saved my life.

I was going through security at the airport. The tinfoil-wrapped heroin in my pocket set off the metal detector. Needless to say, things did not go well. I was arrested. My sister bailed me out on the condition that I go to rehab, and I agreed. After all, I needed to get out of jail so I could get my next hit.

Going to rehab didn't become my true choice—a choice that I owned—until my son saw me grabbing some syringes. We'd stopped by my house so I could pack up some stuff to take with me. I took that opportunity to do as much coke as I could. I had run out of needles, so I went to the kitchen to grab the syringes that we used for our diabetic dog. I had just left jail forty-five minutes before and had two felony charges under my belt, but it didn't matter—Train Wreck was in control. Just as I grabbed the syringes, I looked up and saw Shane, watching me. I put them down and went to rehab.

This was my third significant time in rehab. I don't want to devalue my other times in rehab—every time was significant because it was a version of hope in reluctant action—but this time, I did all of the work, including the work surrounding the emotional pain I had shoved down so deep. It was the hardest thing I've ever done in my life. This was my thought process: *I've done this before. For god's sake, I was sober for ten years. I can do it again, but maybe I can't. . . .* Doubt, fear, and shame were key players in my thinking at this time. Ultimately, I chose hope, because I wanted to live. I slowly moved Train Wreck from the front seat and packed her away to the trunk.

Know thyself. Yes and yes again. But self-knowledge is nothing without action, and that action has to come from the heart. True awareness must journey from the core to create wellness and willingness; it can't just come from the mind. The ways in which I'd previously been using my smartness as the guide to wellness came slowly into focus. I thought, *Well, I'm very smart, so I should be able to master this*, but I came to realize that I needed a deeper knowing than this. The old saying, "the longest journey is from the head to the heart," rings true, I suppose.

I took my five months in rehab to dive deep into my life and to do so with honesty, leaving nothing hidden from myself. I pulled out and examined all of my shame and guilt, all of my grief and anger. I let myself know the truth of my own story. It was a devastating and redemptive process.

I learned about the physiological mechanics of my disorder during this time. I learned about the recovery process, the reasons for each step. For the first time, I holistically informed myself about my disease.

Examining your life and understanding your disease are two of the most important gifts you will ever give yourself. Recovery is ongoing, like life, and neither is frozen in time. Finding the language that defines your addiction allows you to put it into context for yourself as a disease that resides in the brain. It also names it. Naming something makes it real; it starts to put you back in the driver's seat. It makes it harder to act as if it's not there. Once it's named, you can lie to everyone else but you can no longer say to yourself that you didn't know. Let's take a closer look at these two essential things on the road to recovery: defining the disease and naming it.

The National Institute on Drug Abuse has a great, straightforward definition of addiction: addiction is "a chronic, relapsing brain disease that is characterized by compulsive drug seeking and use, despite harmful consequences."[2] When you are examining the definition, really pay attention to the word *compulsive*, because it's key to understanding addiction. It's telling you that no amount of willpower, morality, or being a good person will get your addiction under your control. It's telling you that the disease takes away your control. You do not have power over it in that way, so release that illusion.

We know that some people become addicted while others do not, and that biology and environment are the primary factors involved. We know that younger people whose brains are still developing and people with mental disorders have a higher vulnerability to this disease. Other factors can also play a role: gender, ethnicity, the specific effect of the substance itself, the way it's introduced to the body, when use starts, access and availability, and cost of the substance. All contribute to increasing the risk of becoming addicted.[3]

This doesn't mean that a person who isn't predisposed to addictive behavior can't become physically addicted. Say such a person becomes addicted to prescription pills. They will likely recognize this as a problem and seek help, or make the necessary changes to avoid the problem or break the addiction. Someone who is predisposed to addictive behavior might not do either.

We've defined the disease. Now, let's name it.

There are different thoughts on how we go about naming addiction for ourselves. Maybe. Here's my take on it:

First, it might take you a while to name it for yourself. It might take breaking down the story of your addiction to find the inner dialogue and language you use with yourself that informs what you call your addiction.

One way to go about examining your story is to write it. But very important here: do not start writing your life story without talking to a counselor, particularly if you've experienced childhood abuse or trauma. (I talk more about this in chapter 11.) Writing serves several purposes. First, it identifies your patterns, such as triggering events, followed by behaviors, followed by consequences, followed by short-term abstinence from the drug of choice due to these consequences, followed by toxic thinking, which leads to toxic behaviors, which leads to using again, which sets the whole pattern in motion anew. Second, it identifies where you were responsible and where other factors were at play, such as genetics. Last, it helps to identify the risk factors, patterns, and behaviors that contribute to active addiction. (Oh, did you see a "justification" there to keep on using? [*It's not my fault, it's genetics.*] I thought so. Listen, those things aren't there as never-ending excuses to continue using and being destructive. Rather, they are there to help you see when you need to pay attention and monitor yourself.)

Writing can be very healing. You get to see the whole narrative outside of the context of the inside of your head. You begin to see that it has a beginning and middle, which means it can have an end too. It can motivate you to change. It can also help others who are working with you on your recovery to understand more about how you tick. It can help you to create a longer-term recovery plan. Writing helps you to evaluate things that you may have never really weighed before. The monologue of *Oh my god, all my life I believed this was all my doing. This was all my fault. I was complicit. I created the dysfunction*, becomes a dialogue with yourself through your writing: *Okay, where was that your fault? How is that your fault?* You get an opportunity to reframe and challenge the narrative.

What we're talking about here is self-talk and how we name things. What are we taking on as true? Is it what other people say? How do we learn our self-talk—the stories we tell ourselves about, well, ourselves? Self-talk is often influenced by what society thinks and says, and how society views us, which, in turn, influences how we name things for ourselves. There are many different ways people talk about addiction. Some talk about it from a medical standpoint. Those looking in at it from the outside might talk about it with a judgmental tinge: "Oh, you're just a druggie. You're just an addict." Other terminology abounds: chemical addiction; substance abuse; substance use disorder; addictive disease; having a monster, passenger, sidekick, Train Wreck; and on and on. You don't need to know them all. You just need to know how you talk about it within the context of yourself and your story.

Some people don't want to identify themselves as addicts, which is understandable. It's like the difference between saying, "I am a disabled person" and "I am a person who has a disability." There's identification and there's naming—these are two different things. Identification goes like this: "I am an addict." Naming goes like this: "I have a disorder." Notice the distinction between *I am* and *I have?* It's whatever you want. If you know you're an alcoholic but don't want to go to meetings because you don't want to say, "Hi, my name is So-and-So, and I'm an alcoholic," that's cool. No one can make you say that. Say whatever you want. You can switch it up. Try, "Hi, I'm So-and-So, and I have an alcohol use disorder." That's consistent with the verbiage in the new DSM-5 (*Diagnostic and Statistical Manual of Mental Disorders*, fifth edition): *substance use disorder, alcohol use disorder, cannabis use disorder*.[4] The important part to take away here is that you can find terminology that makes the most sense to you and then use that terminology to name your addiction. If you don't want to identify with a label, that's fine. Find some other way to say it.

There are going to be people who might say, "Oh, well, that one's in denial. That one doesn't want to identify as an alcoholic or an addict," but you know what? Some of the old-timer, 12-step people are going to have an opinion about everything. They might have an opinion about how you dress. They might have an opinion about what you drive, who you hang out with, what you do for a living. They may even have an opinion on how much money you spend on nonfat, no-foam, triple venti lattes at Starbucks. My strong recommendation is to stick with what works best for you. Remember, addiction is idiosyncratic. You've got to find what speaks to you first and foremost.

This road trip isn't about anyone but you. Whatever you call yourself and your addiction, name it in a way that supports your recovery. Learn your story, learn about your disease and the mechanisms behind it, and then name the fucker. Make your addiction real so that you can start to deal with it.

STEP UP

Learn about your substance(s) of choice. Learn about how it acts in your brain. Learn everything that you can about the consequences of using, from physical consequences to emotional ones. If you do decide to do this, take notes (your attention span might be for shit if you've just left detox).

Make a concerted effort to ask questions about how your disorder acts in your brain, such as: How does this disorder affect my sleep? How does it affect my memory? How does it affect my attention span? Google that shit, my friends. Take notes here, too, so you can remember it when you wake up in the middle of the night, craving a hit.

Make knowledge your best friend, and it will support you for life.

IT WORKS IF YOU WORK IT

Think about the various ways people name addiction. Are there terms that rub you the wrong way? Are there terms that make you think, *That's how I view my addiction.* Once you have settled on a name for your addiction, say it out loud: "My name is So-and-so, and I have . . ." Write about how it feels to give your addiction a name.

Bounce Back

On choosing recovery and resilience

The world breaks everyone, and afterward,
some are strong at the broken places.
—Ernest Hemingway

When I was getting high, it felt great. Seriously. Then there were the moments between hits: the need, the compulsion, the desire for the ritual of the needle and the spoon. The underbelly. Never forget the moments in between. This is about getting down to reality—we forget about the need and the fear, followed by the desire to do it all again.

The thing is, it would have felt great right up until it killed me. My last thought, if I were still able to think clearly, would have been, *At least I'm high!* That's how great it felt. And when my addiction was active, there was very little I wouldn't and didn't do to get that feeling as often as I could.

So if it feels so great and you don't care at all about any consequences, why choose recovery?

Maybe because you've got charges pending. Or your parents have thrown you out of the house and you're living in your car. Or you wake up in dread, caught in the rigor of one gigantic craving—brow knitted and body stretched so taut that it feels like you might shatter at any moment—and all you are thinking about is the next shot, the next drink, the next hit. You choose recovery because, otherwise, it's a living death.

You choose recovery because you find a moment when you say, "Oh my god, I can't live this way anymore." Or you say, "Mom, I'm done, and I think I'm dying. I'm going to die here. I'm high, and I have abscesses on my arms."

Then they come and they scoop you up, get you into treatment, and you think, *Oh, fuck. This isn't what I wanted. I just wanted to feel better in that moment. It really wasn't that bad. I wasn't really that bad. I'm fucking signing out of here. I'm not going to do this anymore.* You think those thoughts even as you detox and see your behavior, even as you take a moment and look back at the scene that you were in and you get that it was a very bad scene.

But this is addiction. It's a compulsion that lives in your brain. It can feel as if the drug is almost another being that has consumed you—you *are* coke, you *are* meth, you *are* alcohol. Even a couple of days' distance from it, even seeing the behavior, you still want to go back. That's when you need a really good sponsor and lots of support; or if you're in treatment, a really good counselor and a really good treatment team. Come crunch time, you're going to need someone to meet you where you are and get you back on track.

You need people who will redirect you, realign you to where you come from. People who will ask: What was it like? How did you feel? Where was that going? How would that have ended up if you hadn't picked up that phone? Or if you hadn't gotten arrested? Or if we hadn't talked you down off that third floor balcony?

It slowly comes to you that the consequences of your addiction are unbearable, internally and externally. For some people, the consequences live only in the tangible, like jail time. For others, maybe it's more about the emotional consequences, or maybe it's about some combination of the two. In the end, the biggest consequence is found in what has been lost. *I've lost my connection to who I am. I've compromised the deepest values that are at my core. I've lost my family, my children. I've lost my job and my savings. I've lost my joy and my passion.*

What kind of loss is it when you've sold your body for drug money? What is the toll for the young client who told me, "I sucked dick for drugs"?

The heart breaks and then the heart breaks and then the heart breaks again.

Why choose recovery? Because you can't have a beautiful day with your son or your mother or your lover. You can't have it because the drug controls you. You can't be in the moment to experience the joy of it because all you can think about is your next hit.

Those are some reasons to choose recovery.

Recovery starts with you and a basic acceptance that you have a problem. From there, you find a way to deal with it. This could mean a 12-step program or clinical treatment. At its base, treatment is about applying interventions that help people to stop using whatever their substance of choice is. The goal is to give a person tools and support so that they can have a fulfilling, productive life. Most therapies concentrate on teaching ways to counteract addiction's effects on the brain and behavior—the idea being that if you have the tools to disrupt the mechanisms that drive your addiction, you will then be able to regain control over your life. In short, while your addiction is not curable, it is very treatable.

Treatment comes in all shapes and sizes. It can be found in clinical settings like a rehab center, where you can be either an outpatient or a resident, and it can be found in informal, self-help groups like 12-step programs. What is key in all of this is that your path matches who you are. Recovery is not one size fits all, mostly because addiction acts differently for each person. While certain common risk factors are understood to be a part of the disease, the patterns and behaviors a person develops around their drug use will be singular to them. Further, while certain responses to treatment can be predicted, the pace of recovery can differ from person to person, with some stages taking longer than others or happening in a different order than someone else's. Because it's different for each person, it's important to have check-ins to see how a treatment plan is working, much like patients with other chronic illnesses check in with their doctors, who do a litmus test and adjust therapies to better match the stage of the disease and the symptoms.

I say recovery starts with you because I really think that recovery starts with a person's ability to bounce back—with their resilience. It's the ability to get up the next day and do it all again. But here's the thing: resilience has a spectrum. Some people bounce back from active addiction or relapse faster than others. Some people realign quickly, and some people are highly resistant to change. I don't know whether resilience is based on some sort of chemistry in the brain or some unknowable source. Some people are just more willing to say, "I'm doing it anyway, and I don't care how I feel. I'm going for it."

We live on the spectrum, but I don't believe that we live at a fixed location on that spectrum. People can move themselves; they can increase their ability to bounce back. I believe this because I know it's possible to create a nature that is hopeful and that allows for resilience.

The biggest thing that limits or slows down the ability to recover from crisis is having a negative internal conversation, creating a narrative for ourselves that spirals us down and bars our resilient nature from manifesting.

I'm going to borrow a useful concept from author don Miguel Ruiz. Ideas are "domesticated" into us from childhood, and we carry these ideas with us as though they are true. We're quite often reacting, behaving, and experiencing through an old belief system that we never even agreed to in the first place. If the belief system is one that devalues you, then it's going to block you from shifting your thinking. Part of getting back up is having an understanding that you are valuable and that your life matters.[1]

There's an old story about a family and their special family ham recipe that acts as a good example of how we inherit our beliefs. A mother and daughter are making their family's special holiday ham. They are getting ready to put it in the oven, but before they do, the mom cuts off the ends and tells her daughter, "Never forget to cut off the ends. It's an important step." The girl asks, "Why is it important to cut the ends off the Christmas ham?" The mother replies that it's just something all of the family does whenever they make the ham. Curious, they go to Grandma and ask her why they cut off the ends of the ham. Grandma replies that that's how her mother taught her, but that's no real answer, so they all go to the great-grandma. They say, "Great-Grandma, what is the big mystery of our family ham? Why do we always cut the ends off?" The great-grandma looks at them in surprise and says, "It's the only way I could fit it into the pan."

A tradition can be carried over and over, and we think it holds deep meaning. We think it's really important when, in fact, it's sometimes just nuts and bolts.

I hear this all the time when someone says, "Well, that's just how I am. I've always been that way." If that's where you're at, then take a moment to look back at your story and find out where the "I've always been that way" comes from. *Have* you really *always* been that way, or is this some sort of learned behavior that can be shifted and changed? I think it's really important for people in early recovery, who are more likely to say "Oh, that's just the way I am," to understand that they've been living by an inherited, negative belief but—and this is the important part—they don't have to continue that way.

You can shift your behavior. You can shift the things you think about. You can shift your focus onto something else, and that's really powerful. And because you can do that, I recommend that you assume you have great resilience until proven otherwise. Have faith, even if you doubt. Do it, even if you don't know that you can.

Someone recently asked me what my favorite part of my recovery is. My answer was simple: everything. It's being alive. It's getting to have a purpose. It's going to work and getting to use what I was talking to the dog about last night, to use my experiences, to maybe shine a light on someone else's behavior so that they can see more clearly what the next thing to do is. It's knowing I can look my son, Shane, in the eye and not feel like there's some part of me that I have to hide from him. It's being able to be present and experience life with my son. It's going to an Indian buffet every weekend with him. It's sitting in our booth, with its leather seats and scratched-up table, and ordering Aloo Masala and looking at each other when we take the first bite because it's *so* good. It's looking at each other and saying, simultaneously, "Oh, potato!"

This one time when we were there, we were talking about something silly. I can't even remember how it happened. Whatever it was, we came up with this song that goes, "Robot, telephone call. Eh, eh, eh, eh, eh. Robot, telephone call." Now, if I look at Shane and I say, "Robot, telephone call," we burst into laughter. It's the funniest thing in the world to us, and nobody else knows what it means; it's just one of those moments you have that connect you. It's just silly and fun and real.

None of that would have happened if I weren't in recovery. I would not be present enough to love these moments, to feel the joy, to see Shane as himself, and to be wholly and completely and sincerely with him.

That is what my recovery looks like.

Recovery is having a life.

To get to your own recovered life, there are some key things to think about, and you need to have a come-to-whoever-your-deity-is conversation with yourself about getting sober.

First, you have to do the work. No bullshit. Listen to those who know and just do it. In early recovery, the worst thing you can do, outside of using, is to overthink everything. Let the process flow.

Second, you need to know there's a difference between doing something by rote and being present so that you can experience your process. Being mindful is paramount.

Third, you must accept that the situation is what it is. You can't go back and change anything. This is where you are. Accept it. This is somewhat pragmatic, but there you go. There is this great section in the Big Book—the primary book used by AA—that goes: "Until I could accept my [addiction], I could not stay sober. Unless I accept life completely on life's terms, I cannot be happy. I need to concentrate not so much on what needs to be changed in the world as on what needs to be changed in me and my attitudes."[2] Just take that in and say amen, because it's God's honest reality of how life works. Life is what it is, and the only thing you can control is how you choose to see it and how you choose to see yourself.

Lastly, you need to remember that recovery is self-determined. There are two aspects to this. There's the physical: anybody can put the plug in the jug, break the tip off the needle, crush the pipe under your heel. That's physical sobriety. That's abstinence. The second aspect is everything else beyond the physical. Recovery begins whenever you let it. You can just be physically abstinent and hope for the best, or you can embrace being fully self-determined and self-motivated. Russel Brand wrote a great article for the *Spectator*, a UK-based magazine, titled "The Only Way to Help Addicts is to Treat Them Not as Bad People but as Sick People." He put it perfectly: "The fact is . . . that the sufferer must be a willing participant in their own recovery. They must not pick up a drink or drug. Just don't pick it up—that's all."[3]

Someone can show you how to get through twenty-four hours without your substance in a controlled environment. They can give you tools and explain the practical application of those tools. But once you walk out the door, what you do with that knowledge will determine your ability to remain in recovery. There's a huge difference between abstinence and recovery. It's a shade of grey but also a spiritual, internal shift that occurs.

In the same way you can break a bone and it will knit back together, you can recover from the injury done to you by your addiction. It takes time, it takes healing, and it takes resilience—plus a little faith.

I used to wake up from drug dreams, and I would have to look over at my bedside table to make sure there was no drug paraphernalia there, because my subconscious was still so directed toward that thinking and habit.

I woke up from a drug dream about six months ago, and my first thought was (because sometimes you wake up and you think it's real, right?), *Why would I do that? My life is so great now, so why would I have done that?* I knew right away that the dream was not real and that I could breathe through it.

Waking up and looking to make sure it wasn't real is one thing; waking up and thinking, *There's no way*, is another thing entirely. It's a shift in consciousness. It's a leap in the right direction. It's the heart of recovery.

You can't talk about recovery without talking about hope. Hope and resilience walk arm in arm. Hope whispers to you and tells you that you have grace, that you are a valuable soul, that you are deserving of love and redemption. It tells you that all things are possible, including recovery, even—and especially—when it seems like nothing is possible at all. Hope, for all that it flutters and whispers and lives inside you, is a bigger thing than you. I believe it is the thing we all must surrender to in the end.

When I hold still, I can hear hope telling me beautiful things. If you hold still, you can too.

SOMETHING TO CONSIDER

You might have heard people say, "Relapse is a part of recovery." I'd like to challenge that and say that relapse is a part of the disease. Relapses happen; it's the nature of the disorder—the chronic part. Don't get stuck thinking about the failure. Instead, self-determine the crap out of your comeback, cultivate your resilience, and bounce back. Repeat until it sticks.

IT WORKS IF YOU WORK IT

Write about a time in your life when you showed great resilience to achieve a goal. How did it feel? How did you push past wanting to give up? When you feel your motivation to recover slipping, return to this time in your mind and remind yourself how resilient you can be.

Here. Now.

On becoming mindful

No one saves us but ourselves. No one can and no one may.
We ourselves must walk the path.

—**Buddha**

Being mindful of the moment matters; it's how we ground our-selves. If you are aware of your present moment and hold on to that awareness, it leaves no room to fixate on the compulsion to go and get high or drunk.

The other day, I looked at the clock on the wall in my office, just a glance to get the time. It struck me as I watched the second hand tick past the minute hand and then the hour hand that the second hand was oddly like an addict when they're using—never staying still, always moving to the next moment.

Need my next hit. *Tick*. I'm a horrible person. *Tick*. How do I get my next hit? *Tick*. God, I'm worthless. *Tick*. Need a hit. *Tick*. Need. *Tick*. Need. Need. Need.

That need and that negative self-talk take up the seconds and the minutes and the hours of an addict's life—hours that head into days and weeks and months and years. And always in a circle, never getting anywhere, never moving forward. That's when you're living your life in time with the second hand. At least the second hand on the clock marks the passing of time, even if it's going in circles.

I began to think more about that clock and about that contrast between that second hand and the other two hands, the minute and the hour. The minute hand pauses briefly, notices its surroundings, takes a quick breath, and then moves on. The hour hand stops and rests, takes in the world. The hour hand breathes deeply. That space between minutes and hours is where life is really lived. It's there where you fill the moments of your life with things that allow the journey around the clock to expand with joy and grief, and all of the other things that make us wise.

When you're deep in addiction, the minute and the hour might as well not even exist. That's how distorted perception and time are when you're using. You're never in the actual moment that you're liv-ing. Your thoughts won't let you be in the here and now; they're too full of compulsive need—too busy telling you the story that insists that your compulsion is right and good.

After I had gotten arrested for possession, I remember saying to the cops, "I'm somebody's mom. I'm somebody's mom. Shane doesn't know. Shane doesn't know," as I was riding around in the back of the cop car for a billion years—okay, it was actually twenty minutes—with my hands cuffed behind my back. That twenty minutes felt like a billion years because I was thinking in terms of me trying to get through the next ten seconds, and the next ten seconds, and then the next ten seconds. The entire time, I was never thinking of where I was right then—not in the cop car, not when I made bail, not when I got on the plane, not when I got to the rehab center. There was no knowing. There was only *What's next?* intermixed with shame. *How am I going to survive this? I need a hit. How do I keep breathing? Oh god, I'm not going to be able to get a hit. I'm a bad mom. Shane doesn't know. I'm a piece of shit.*

When you're in recovery, you have to work to ground yourself in what is in the moment you are currently in. You have to work the quiet and then begin to change the negative self-talk. Mindfulness of the moment—allowing the moment to be what it is—is hard to inhabit. To make it a natural impulse, you have to practice.

I'm not necessarily talking about meditation, although that can certainly help. I'm talking about an internal shift of consciousness and the willingness to really be present. To be intimate with the details of where you are right now, to really pay attention to the person you are with, to breath mindfully, and to acknowledge that you are here and now.

You can do this physically. For example, make a fist and squeeze it tight. Really squeeze. Hold that squeeze, stop reading for a moment, and pay attention to it—then come back, still holding the squeeze.

Do you feel how your forearm tenses, how your nails bite a little into your palm? Do you feel the strain as you clench your fingers? The stretch in your skin at the joints?

Release it. Feel the difference?

Hyperaware of your hand right now, aren't you? There you go: you just grounded in the moment. Your whole mind was aimed at feeling your hand clench and then release. What else were you thinking about when you concentrated on the sensations of clenching your hand? Probably nothing. And now you're going to be super aware of your hand for a while after this little exercise. (Sorry about that.)

You can do this exercise systematically by clenching and releasing the muscles in different parts of your body, or by simply focusing on different body parts one at a time and then moving on. It's a good way to self-soothe if you're feeling anxious or if your thoughts just won't settle.

Another way to work on being aware of the moment is to take a minute or two to describe your surroundings to yourself, or to describe to yourself exactly what you're doing in that moment in time. Have you ever described your day to yourself? Here's one of mine:

In the morning, in that moment when I wake up, that's the moment I try to bring myself into first thing. *This is my bed. The light is beautiful coming through the window. My dogs are curled around me on the bed—I love you, puppies! My cat sounds like she's in utter despair. I should feed her now.*

I think, *Thank you, God, for my beautiful life. Thank you for another day. Thank you for the opportunity to make progress and to be healthy and strong.* Then a chihuahua or a pug starts licking a part of my face, and I think, *Yeah, yeah, I get it. Stay humble. I'll stay humble and just keep putting one foot in front of the other.*

I get up, go into the bathroom, rinse my mouth, and pee. I wash my hands and head downstairs. Let the dogs out. I start to assemble the day in my mind as I'm heading toward the kitchen. I have a grind-and-brew machine, so I always have that yummy aroma of coffee surrounding me in the morning. I pour my cup. I pay attention to where I am and what I'm doing as I'm fixing my coffee: one teaspoon of raw sugar and vitamin D milk (the thick organic kind).

One of the dogs needs medicine. They all need their herbs. They need their food, and they need to go outside and pee before they destroy the house. As I sip through my first cup, I try and prioritize what I'm going to need to do for the day. Is it a day where I'm leading a group or am I just going straight into client sessions? I pause as I consider, just to continue to focus and get grounded.

I continue to check in with myself throughout my day—every day—in this manner. If I feel myself floating off into worry or anxiety or distraction, I bring it back to the small details, reground myself, and then move forward.

Another type of mindfulness is to be aware of the words you use, the way you phrase things. Do you phrase things always as either/or? Are the word choices you choose always negative? Are you compassionate with how you describe yourself to yourself? Do you use language that lifts you up or pulls you down?

Language and how we choose to use it is powerful. We can use it to bludgeon ourselves into an emotional pulp or we can use it to open ourselves up to new and wonderful things. When you tell your story, listen for repeated phrases and words. The words you use to tell your story will also tell you about your self-talk and your perceptions of the world.

Mindfulness is one of the most effective behavioral tools you will ever have for dealing with rising anxiety, stress, sadness, and myriad other emotions that can start you on a downward spiral of negative thinking. It's a healthy way to self-soothe that is about a gazillion times better than that other way you've been self-soothing. (*Ding, ding, ding!* Drugs and/or alcohol.)

If you are practicing sensory mindfulness (being bodily and environmentally aware), it can make things real in a way that offers you a deep connection with the world. Take a drive or go on a hike, and do it like you're embarking on a life-changing journey because, hey, you are. Go east in the morning and west in the afternoon— pursue the sun. Look around you and *be* where you are.

There is a trail I know of with evergreens bracketing the sides. They stand like beautiful mystics, frocked in green. Their trunks and branches stretch up as if in praise of the sun or the sky, or maybe God. They make a cathedral out of the trail. I like to find a place to sit and then take everything in, listen to the birds; and stay long enough to watch the lengthening shadows mark the passing of time like the gliding minute and hour hands of a giant clock.

Mindfulness gives back the moments that you would have otherwise never noticed. The distortion of time, the negative perception of self and the world, steals wonder from you. It takes away the joy of gratitude. Mindfulness helps you get it back—it's always the goal.

Internal mindfulness—which is to say mindfulness that pays attention to negative self-talk—watches for negative patterns of behavior and perceptions. It takes some doing because you have to break through the distortion of what you think versus what is true. You might be thinking, *Everyone is out to get me!* But is it actually true? Break it down. Do you know everyone in the world? No? Then what you're thinking isn't true. If you are thinking you're worthless, ask yourself how you'd go about figuring out if that's true. Treat it like a hypothesis. Do the facts support the claim? Have you ever made someone feel better with a hug? If so, you had worth to that person. Therefore, you aren't worthless. Challenge the shit out of your habitual thoughts and behaviors. Ask, *Why do I think that? Why do I do that?* Get mindful about what's real and what's distorted.

Addicts use all-or-nothing thinking: everything's shit or everything's beautiful. We rarely walk the middle road. Negative thoughts can creep in even if you're in the middle of doing the most beautiful, sober-as-fuck activity out there. Here's the deal: you could get rid of the drugs and get rid of the alcohol, but if you don't work on your thought processes, you're not going to make a ton of progress. You're not going to be happy.

If addiction is a disease of distorted perception and negative thought processes, then you're not left with a drinking problem; you're left with a thinking problem. Many of us are constantly talking to ourselves in negative ways, but we don't fully realize it. This negative self-talk lives below the level of consciousness, so we're not aware that we're doing it until we begin the practice of self-monitoring and self-intervention.

Say you're watching Animal Planet one night—a show about big predators on the African plains. There's a herd of gazelles running around in perfect formation. They're leaping along, and they're all happy and safe. But then there's that one little shit that inevitably runs away from the herd, right? One second, he's safe in the middle, and the next, he's broken off from the group because he's not paying attention. We all know what happens next. Say hello to the lions, little buddy! But you can control those gazelle thoughts; you just have to recognize them for what they are and get them back in line before the lions close in for the kill.

In the end, mindfulness demands acceptance of what *is*. You can't be mindful and regretful at the same time. You can be mindful of the regret, but the regret is not being *felt*—being seen and being acknowledged, yes, but not felt. As you practice mindfulness, you'll notice that your ability to accept what you can't change gets easier. Through the doing comes the being.

Practice mindfulness and let the rest flow through.

Mindfulness is indeed a practice, and like every other thing that takes practice, you have to work at it. Sometimes you'll be on your A game and sometimes not so much. And when it's not so much, it sucks. A thousand days can be lived in a bad night when you toss and turn because you can't shake shit loose. You want to say, "Fuck mindfulness! Nothing is okay. Nothing works." In these moments, try being like water. Think of a river with boulders and rocks, logs and reeds. The water doesn't stop when it encounters these things; it comes up and against, slides around, and goes through. Be like water. Ride through it; don't fight it. Reach for hope. Remember the clock hands—the minute and the hour. Find the breath between one moment and the next, even if your second-hand thoughts and negative self-talk are trying to take over.

At the end of my day, as I'm lying in my bed happy, falling asleep, I'll go over my day in my mind. I'll look at who I interacted with and what my interactions were like—where I was selfish, where I was intolerant, where I was impatient, where I was defiant. I make note to be mindful of those things the next day, to raise the bar, to make amends where I need to set something right. Then I release it. I focus on sensation, on the moment I am in. I feel how comfy my bed is and listen to the night sounds of my house. I fall into my body in that time and in that space. Honestly, it feels like those trees on that trail. It feels like I am stretching upward, like I'm a cathedral.

SOME FINAL THOUGHTS ON MINDFULNESS

Remember, addiction is personal and so is recovery. If you're trying to become mindful and the method you're using doesn't work, experiment with other methods until you find one that works for you. But don't wait for this to happen to you. Make a beginning. Get into motion.

IT WORKS IF YOU WORK IT

Practice mindfulness by finding a place where you can comfortably sit and close your eyes for five minutes. (This can be indoors or outdoors.) With your eyes closed—no peeking!—pay attention to all the sounds around you. Name them in your mind as you hear them: *meowing cat, driving car, wind in the branches*. When the five minutes are over, notice how much more connected you feel to the place where you are than you did when you first sat down. You might be surprised at how much your perception changes when beginning to practice mindfulness. There is a world of possibility, and, if you are willing to try, it's there to be experienced.

4

Leaping Like Kierkegaard

On trusting yourself and on others

trusting you

Stop acting so small;
you are the universe in ecstatic motion.

—Rumi

I've been leaping most of my life—leaping to trust, to a higher power (God, the universe, or whatever you want to call it), and to hope. I'm leaping to those three things pretty much all of the time. Most people take a leap *of* faith. I like both: *of* and *to*. There is a difference between a leap *of* something and a leap *to* something. When I say I'm leaping *to* something like hope, I mean I'm making a leap *in the direction of* hope. When I say I'm taking a leap *of* hope, it means I already know and believe that hope exists (it's already inside me). Sometimes it's the first version of leaping, sometimes it's the second. I do both every day. Every day I'm leaping—that's me, in midair. When I am leaping and when I think about what that truly means, it's kind of breathtaking.

We all do it—I mean, shit, I wake up and think, *I hope I have a good day*. Leap! Sometimes it's with my eyes squeezed shut and holding my breath, like when I jump into a cold pool. Sometimes it's with my eyes wide open, laughing out loud, like when I jump on a trampoline.

Think of the movement of leaping. Our muscles tense, and our knees bend a little in preparation as the body shifts forward onto the toes. For a moment, all of our weight is held there in a coiled position, the moment before action. If we stay too long on our toes, we start to wobble—it's a precarious place to be, on your toes, before you leap. I've always wondered how people stay in that position. Leap already! You're coiled up for the spring, so do it!

Once you've put yourself in motion, you are more likely to continue to move forward. Think about the motion of objects: If an object isn't in motion, it's very difficult to motivate it to move—it wants to stay put. But if it's already in motion, you can gently guide and motivate it along the path that it needs to go on. Likewise, once you get into motion, it's easier to follow direction. It's easier to change. If you're at rest and you're just static, not doing anything, it's very difficult to motivate yourself into action. When you start taking action, however, going forward becomes easier. If you're in motion, it's going be a lot harder to stop you than if you're sitting still.

Moving toward recovery is a do-or-don't kind of situation. Recovery requires, demands, wants, *needs* choice and action. If you go for it, you will be able to continue to go forward unless stopped by something else. If you stay static, if you stay on the fence, I guarantee that you'll fall, and it won't be into recovery. And when we hit the ground, the consequences usually include something being broken— you know, like your spirit, your heart, your body, your mind.

When you've chosen to leap, all of the motion happens at once: the release of your energy *and* the extension of your limbs *and* the flight forward, upward. Everyone does it differently, some with wild abandon, arms flailing and legs pumping in the air, and giant hoots and hollers. Some do it headfirst, a quick streamlined dive like a lifeguard off of a platform. Some pull their arms close to their bodies, cross their feet at the ankles, scream, and maybe they plug their nose too—they're waiting to be enveloped from the feet up by the consequences of their actions.

I think all leaps are beautiful; it's the moment of choice that matters most. Then when you jump, you rise up, and for the briefest of moments, you feel like you're suspended there. It's like a gasp of wonder mixed with fear. You're in anticipation—you've surrendered to not knowing.

Many years ago—the late nineties—I was sharing a house with a friend. It was a small house. I had just moved back to California after living in the mountains in Pennsylvania for years. I was going to recapture my acting career. Then my roommate decided he wanted to move. *Oh my god, where am I going to come up with $1,500 a month?* I thought. But instead of deciding to squeeze myself into a tiny box apartment somewhere, I said to myself, *I'm taking a leap of faith. I'm just going to believe that I'll be able to handle this in a smart way.* I just believed that I was in a good enough position that it would have to work out. This doesn't happen for everybody, but two weeks later, I booked a series on the Disney Channel. Things worked out. If they hadn't worked out, however, I simply would have reassessed. I would have adjusted my course.

There's a Springsteen song called "Leap of Faith" that says, "It takes a leap of faith to get things going." That always resonated with me, because if we don't leap—even when it's scary as hell and even when we don't know where we're going to land—then we spend our lives never moving forward.

Do we ever land? Sometimes we do. And when we land, it's an awesome landing.

After I got arrested and was in rehab, a family member came to visit me in Louisiana at the rehab facility. We were sitting together in the visiting area and he said, "Look, you're going to have to sell your house. You're facing these charges. You're in rehab. You have this expensive house. You need to sell your house." I remember sitting there in the pretend family room, taking those words in, and I knew, somewhere deep within myself, that I was going to be capable of rising like a phoenix.

I said, "No, I don't. I don't need to sell my house. I can come back from this. I don't have to give up my home that I've had for a decade because you think that I'm not going to be able to pull this off." That was a leap of faith; I leapt because I believed in myself and my capacity to recover. I kept my house, and I'm sitting in it right now. It was hard work to do it, but I just knew that I would and could. *Leap*.

This is not something to overthink. Overthinking is the great leap killer, the momentum stopper. We often get overwhelmed when we think about risk, and jumping into the unknown always feels like a risk. We choke with thought and are unable to move, to make the jump. The mind tells us the leap is unsafe, and we don't take action because we're busy considering what our mind is telling us about the leap instead of taking it. The mind is right; taking action is scary.

And why wouldn't it be? When you're in action, you've taken off but haven't landed anywhere yet.

When you've put yourself in motion, you're in the space between where you were and where you're going. Once you've made a decision to leap, you're in the moment of flight and are no longer asking, "Should I do it?" You're in the middle of the answer, and you're hoping like hell you got it right but kind of already feel like you did. It's a crazy amount of trust in and surrender to the universe. You leap and then think, *Please, please, please, Universe, don't screw me*, followed by, *But I kind of don't think you will*. This is a leap of faith and a leap to hope.

Early recovery is a series of huge leaps. It starts with the moment of crisis—external and internal—that brought you here and made you say, "This is my tipping point. I'm either going to fall or leap." Somewhere along the way, you decided to leap.

Imagine there is a deep canyon with fog rising up from its floor. You are standing on one side of this canyon. You don't know how deep the canyon is, and you can't see the edge of the other side through the blanket of fog. What you do know is that it's dangerous on this side of the canyon, and getting to the other side is the only way you'll get away from the danger. You have three options: you can stand there and think about it, you can go back toward the danger, or you can jump to the other side. Imagine you choose to take the chance. You leap.

Using your mind's eye, imagine taking a leap from your edge toward the other side of the canyon. Imagine yourself reaching for the other side. *Really* imagine it. Your arms are outstretched and your heart is in your throat. You are leaping with the hope that you will make it to the other side but also without any type of guarantee that you will find steady footing when you land.

But here's the weird thing: not knowing doesn't matter as you hang suspended, because you are fully free in that moment. You've made that decision and taken action; you have released the before and not yet captured the after; you are weighed down by nothing. In this moment is the relief of grace. You're okay with the fact that you don't know what's going to happen next, and you inexplicably know that you can trust that no matter how you land, you can do whatever is next. There is something in you that tells you that you can manage that landing and that, to paraphrase Bob Marley, everything's going to be alright. It's an amazing feeling.

One more thing about leaping before we move on: don't just go leaping off a cliff all willy-nilly. Talk to people about it. Do a little research. Make educated leaps as much as possible. You feel me? Because the reality is that we don't land perfectly every time. Sometimes we miss the mark and land in a pile of shit. But it doesn't mean we've failed. It just means that there was a pile of shit there and we should avoid that spot next time.

I've had a leap (or two) that's gone bad before. When I got out of rehab in 2008, my car was a piece of crap—it kept breaking down. I knew I needed to get another one, but I didn't have money and my credit was bad. So I went to a dealership where my mom's neighbor worked (yes, it's one of *those* stories). I went to the dealership and was presented with a deal on a Jaguar that was awesome—the kind of awesome that is the too-good-to-be-true awesome. (And the little voice in my head knew it too.) But I decided to take a leap of faith that everything was on the up and up. I bought the car and, of course, Karmageddon ensued.

Really, what *wasn't* wrong with it was the question. Almost immediately, it started overheating and would stall out in the worst places ever. Intersections and dark, lonely highways in the middle of the night seemed to be the locales of choice. Coolant regularly erupted and spewed all over the place every time I popped the hood. My car was like Mount Vesuvius on wheels. It was miserable. Then I got stranded out in the middle of nowhere—and by nowhere, I mean no-cell-service nowhere. I thought about walking but nixed that idea. Then this Mexican guy in a pickup truck stopped to help. He took a look at my engine and declared that the coolant hose had a major leak. He had a case of water in the back of his truck, and he gave it to me, saying "Pour water in there and get to a gas station." That was it, I was done. Finally, after sucking it up for two years, I waved a white flag and admitted that the car was a POS, a total lemon. Leaping lesson learned.

When I made the decision to go back to school, that was an informed leap. It was still scary as shit, but it was a decision I'd made for myself after doing some research and asking lots and lots of questions; I was going to own it. Shopping for pens and sticky notes took me back to the excitement of my childhood and the back-to-school shopping trips I shared with my mom. Even if I was the oldest person in the room and even if I was scared I'd fail, I'd made my choice. And now it was time to jump in and try to move forward. That leap was a success.

Okay, I just covered a lot of ground there. Trust and lack thereof, hope, the universe (with some surrender to uncertainty thrown in there too), and a lot of leaping toward trust. But it's important leaping, so let's look more at what the trust we're leaping toward looks like.

I'll start with trusting the process. To be blunt, everyone who's working with you, who's helping you recover, they know better than you when you first start the recovery process. Hard to believe, right? They even know you better than *you*. There's an element of trusting the people that went before you, who have lived through what you are living through and trusted the process of recovery. For instance, I know that if I'm actively working on my recovery, I'll stay clean.

It's a starting point for my recovery. I make a leap of trust every day, putting my heart into it.

You have to be present. Even if you've done it before and you think you know everything about it, you've got to set aside everything you think you know and allow yourself to have a completely new experience. That is a huge exercise in trust. If you have to, close your eyes but still jump toward these people. They're reaching out their arms to grab you—to catch you when you think you're going to fall instead of landing on solid ground. It's okay to be scared. We all are.

Now, self-trust, that's a biggie. Allowing yourself to trust yourself is a process like everything else, and it happens really quickly for some people and really slowly for others. But no matter what, it usually starts with others helping you identify good and bad choices when it comes to being around or in situations that aren't safe for where you are in the recovery process.

Think of the self-trust process like this: You've been invited to this dinner party, but oh man, you know there are going to be some really nice bottles of wine there. That's when other people's assessment comes into play. That's where you call your trusted advisor, your sponsor, your therapist, your counselor. These people are probably going to say something like, "Yeah . . . that's a bad idea," or they'll recommend you take another sober friend with you who can help you get out of the situation if it becomes too difficult to manage. It's about learning how to assess a situation with wisdom that others have from their own experiences. It's riding a bike with the training wheels on. It's jumping out of a plane tandem. There are dozens of analogies I can make here, but they're all getting at the same fundamental point.

To trust yourself fully you have to know in your soul that you've altered your negative behaviors into safe and healthy behaviors. This means you have to do the work. Mastering behaviors is all about training and repetition. For instance, create a list of questions you should ask yourself before you decide something, then go down that list when you need to make a decision. Every. Time. What you are creating is the *of* here—the known platform. A leap *of* trust while you leap to faith. Trust happens over time and with consistent actions.

This doesn't mean you trust that you will be able to fix everything all of the time. That's not going to happen because you're not perfect—none of us are. What it's about is trusting in your ability to navigate and manage the bumps in your road. You have that power.

One of the bumps you'll hit almost instantly during recovery is others asking, "Can I trust you?" Going back to my early rehab days, I remember thinking, *Everyone should trust me immediately again because look what I've done! I've gotten sober. Gold stars all around!* But I always have to remind myself—and remind my clients too— that you have to earn that trust. And that's okay.

There's an acronym that I use during this stage of the process: TIME, or Trust I Must Earn. Trust takes time. You have to earn it back, and so the thought process of *Look at me, I'm sober. I made it to thirty days. Why are they all still looking at me funny? Don't they trust me?* isn't actually serving you well. Look at your track record. It's going to take a lot longer than thirty days. It takes time, and it takes a continuum of behaviors to re-establish trust with yourself and with the people in your life. The people who love you are probably thinking, *Don't tell me what you're going to do,* show *me what you're going to do. Then maybe I'll begin to trust you.*

You may feel pretty smart and capable after a short time being sober, but the truth is that you have to examine your track record— both through your own eyes and through the eyes of the people in your life. Give both yourself and your people the time to establish trust again. Show yourself and them this process toward recovery, don't just tell. And never discount the value of a second opinion.

Alina Lodge, the rehab center I went to that gave me the skills to stay sober for ten years, was run by an eighty-five-year-old woman who had been sober for forty-five years by then. Her name's Mrs. Delaney. I was at this center for nine months, and Mrs. Delaney rode me so hard. She rode everybody hard, but me in particular.

You don't graduate from this center when you think you are ready but when *they* think you are ready. Some people stayed a year, a year and a half. When someone graduates from this program, they get a keychain. I still have mine.

When it was time to get my coveted keychain, I went into Mrs. Delaney's office. This lady had drawn-on eyebrows, crooked lipstick—I worshiped this woman. She was a force of nature. She looked me square in the eyes and said, "Why do you think you're in my office?" I replied, "Because I can leave? Because it's over? Because I can go?" Mrs. Delaney had my keychain in her hand. She fixed me with this look and said, "Don't tell me how ready you are. I'm from the 'show me' state. So get out there and show me."

That was huge for me. It was just one of those moments you never forget. So I went out and I showed her. I went on to become a member of the board of Alina Lodge. I went on to be able to sit at her table during lunch when I would come back to visit. All through the time I was in rehab, I thought, *One day I'm going to sit at that table with Mrs. Delaney and have lunch.*

Let me explain. When I was at Alina Lodge for all those months, there was a staff table. Visiting counselors and recovered patients sat at that table with Mrs. Delaney and the rest of the staff. It was this big, round table, and it had a big lazy Susan in the middle. On that lazy Susan was tomato jam. I'd never had tomato jam. Tomato jam just seemed not right. But the more I thought about it, the more I really wanted to taste it. There were all these different condiments on the lazy Susan, though none as exotic as the tomato jam. I would watch as the staff would spin the lazy Susan around. All the staff members would be laughing and talking, and Mrs. Delaney would be holding court. Meanwhile, I was at the rehab table, sans tomato jam.

I made up my mind that one day I was going to sit at that table with Mrs. Delaney and the staff, on a level playing field, and I was going to be able to have some damn tomato jam, whatever that hell that is and whatever the hell it tastes like. I would know.

To do that, I had to work my recovery. I had to get well. It was a small thing as a motivator, but I would remind myself about it when I was having a bad day: "Remember, Mack, this is the path to that tomato jam."

And then one day, after I'd been discharged, Mrs. Delaney invited me back to the lodge for lunch. I got to sit at that table, and I got to spin the lazy Susan like a roulette wheel until that tomato jam landed right in front of me. And I ate it, and it was good. It tasted like victory!

I got to do that because I didn't just tell Mrs. Delany that I was ready and trustworthy, I showed her through consistent work.

Trust is surrendering to something outside of your control. There is an almost unnameable shift to make. Some might call it a spiritual shift—I do. You will need to find your own words for it, but the truth of this remains: making leaps of trust and leaps to faith both involve a huge amount of uncertainty and letting go.

Let's talk a little more about faith and the spiritual shift of releasing control to a greater something, a higher power. What that higher power is, in my mind, is a personal understanding. For me, your higher power can be the look of love in your dog's eyes. It can be spying a beautiful wild horse running on the beach—it doesn't have to be a deity. It just has to be something external that's more powerful than you. I would like the sun to set in the east tonight. Can I manifest that miracle? I cannot; therefore, nature is a power greater than me, and nature can be my higher power.

Let me preface this next bit by saying I'm really not that much of a Bible person, but man, does it have some great bites of wisdom!

There's this quote from the Bible, the book of Mark, that goes something like, "I do believe! Help my unbelief."[1] The reason I like this is because it's saying that once we shout, "Yes, this is what I believe!" we're proclaiming we've done it, even if we still doubt sometimes; even if we have to suspend our disbelief. It's saying that, whatever your higher power is, it is there waiting for you, no matter what. It doesn't matter if you believe or don't believe; it's there even when you feel like you don't have any faith left at all.

There's a part of me that gets turned off by specifying God with a capital G, (as in God, the Creator), but there is also a part of me that feels the pull toward speaking to something outside myself when I need to as part of my recovery process. His Holiness the Dalai Lama said: "This is my simple religion. There is no need for temples; no need for complicated philosophy. Our own brain, our own heart is our temple; the philosophy is kindness."[2] I don't know if God created the universe and everything in it, but I do know that I want to get well so badly that I will seek and find him or a version of the universe. Eventually, I will align with some idea of a power outside of myself to whom I can say, "Please help me. I'm crazy. I'm unhappy. Nothing is satisfying me. Please show me." In some ways, we're talking to the power outside of ourselves when we do this, and at the same time, we're also talking to ourselves. It's like speaking simultaneously to the universe—to God or your version of God, whatever or whoever that may be—as well as to your inner instinct, your soul, or your spirit; that part of you that answers when you ask for guidance.

Maybe when we do this we're all speaking to the hope and the trust inherent in a leap of faith. I don't know how it works, but I don't need to know to surrender to this part of the process. Trust is there when I pray, when I ask for peace and surrender and serenity, and when I feel I'm out of balance. Trust is there when I ask for help from my friends and from a higher power alike. Trust is there when I ask for help from deep within myself at every stage of my ongoing journey of recovery. It's even sometimes in a pause and when I go, *Oh! Yeah, that*. Simple things like, "Oh my god, my entire body is wound tight," and I say, "Please, just give me the opportunity to relax." It's a sense of something bigger that is outside of myself but that I can feel inside myself, in the place I would call my soul, my spirit.

While trust does contain a huge element of uncertainty and the giving up of control, what you can control is your thoughts—no more of the *Oh, that's just the way I am* complacency that so many of us get used to when we try to justify behaviors and choices we're not so proud of. If that's what you fall back on when you're trying to explain why you can't stick with recovery, I've got to ask, how's that working out for you? I bet not so great. Remember our discussion on mindfulness and positive self-talk in chapter 3? Never is this more important than when you're taking a leap to and of trust.

As we close out our look into faith, trust, and embracing the leap to and of recovery, I want to mention the man in the title of this chapter, the nineteenth century philosopher Søren Kierkegaard. What on earth does a dead Danish guy have to do with recovery? For one, he had some great things to say about taking leaps of faith.

Kierkegaard maintained that belief was reserved for things that could be proven, and faith was for the territory of things that couldn't but were no less important—like God.[3] Can we prove beyond a shadow of a doubt that God exists? Nope. Do we need to in order to have faith and for that faith to be a transformative force of good in our lives? Nope.

Kierkegaard thought of God as something beyond logic and outside of empirical proof. He also argued that, in order for faith to mean anything, we have to constantly ask ourselves what faith means to us in the everyday context of living and then choose faith over and over again, even when it's hard to do so.[4] In this way, taking the leap of and to recovery is like having faith in God. We can't know for sure what's waiting for us on the other side, but if we never try—if we never have faith in ourselves and in the powers that surround us—we'll never know.

FOR GOD'S SAKE, LEAP!

Here are four things for your leaping consideration:

Leap toward change.

Leap into surrender.

Leap to trust.

Leap to hope.

IT WORKS IF YOU WORK IT

Is there an area in your life where you need to take a leap? Instead of focusing on the unknown, take some time to write about what will happen if you don't leap. For example, what would happen if you chose to stay working in an unhealthy environment instead of finding a new job or going back to school? Is the unknown really worse than the known? Now write about all the potential good that could come from your leap. There's no guarantee of those good outcomes, but there is a guarantee of the negative ones that will happen if you stay put, without making any changes for the better. Either way, you'll have to leap.

Surrender to the Kittens

On control, acceptance, and surrender

First you take a drink, then the drink takes a drink, then the drink takes you.

—F. Scott Fitzgerald

There are certain things we have no control over—the sun rising, the fact that those large SUVs that start with an H and rhyme with "bummer" are gas guzzlers, and your aunt's inexplicable love of sweatshirts with kittens on them.

I know I just gave you an imaginary aunt with a weird kitty fetish, but go with me on this. My point here is that the sun rises (and even sets), a Bummer guzzles gas, and your aunt's kitty-love? All of these things are what they are, and we accept that we can't change them, no matter how much we want to stop the dawn, fix the ozone, or help Auntie broaden her wardrobe to include something other than kittens (like, say, owls). We understand that these are things we have zero control over.

Your control over things that are outside of *you* is super small, as in nonexistent. Sure, you can do things to influence people, like try to get your aunt to stop wearing kitten sweatshirts, but you can't make her stop loving them. Because it is not in your control. Because it is outside of you. You're not the boss of her. And seriously, do you want to be? Just accept it and surrender to the kittens.

Acceptance and control, control and acceptance—in the world of recovery, these two things are connected and fit into an equation that, when combined with surrender, end up equaling a pretty amazing sense of release.

Of course, telling yourself to surrender is one thing; actually doing it is something else. As with most things, you have to begin somewhere. But what, exactly, is acceptance? The first thing to understand is that acceptance is an action: when we accept something, we are in the act of acknowledging it with an attitude of tolerance and broadmindedness. Acceptance is often connected with letting go, but I like to think about it as consenting to just let something be what it is. And keep this in mind: you don't have to let go of whatever you're trying to accept; it's a part of your life, a part of what makes you *you*—and you should always feel welcome within yourself.

Try just letting the thing be what it is without a running critique and commentary. It's the critique and commentary that keeps the thing front and center. Begin to turn that commentary off, and it recedes, becoming one of the memories that make up the emotional furniture and knickknacks of your inner house.

How do we accept something? If we're talking about past things, the first thing you have to acknowledge is that nothing you do *now* is going to change what happened *then*. Time is all forward motion; there isn't a reverse. The clock doesn't go backward, and neither can you. By picking up a drink or taking a drug, you might think that you can relive the past (hello, *Groundhog Day*). Here's the thing: you could choose to try and relive the same day over and over, or you could choose to not act on your addiction. All you can pretty much do is say, "Well, that happened," and then learn how to move forward. This sucks, and it's hard to do; acceptance of all of the crap things in your past doesn't happen overnight. You have to be mindful of it and practice this acceptance every day. Once you have the motions down, you have to continue to choose it every day. Choosing is powerful.

If we're talking about accepting what's going on right now, the first thing you have to do is acknowledge that now is happening. The next thing—and this is the hardest thing—is to do nothing and take a moment to let the situation be what it is. To do this, you need to be as open-minded as you can. And be mindful, of course. And both take practice.

Acceptance is not saying that you can't change. It's not saying, "This is how it is; this is how it's always going to be." It means that you have come to experience a peace with things as they are without taking away the ability to create change. You're not saying, "I give up." What you're doing is acknowledging that you can't change the nature of your substance use disorder—that if you have the first drink or the first shot, that if you pick it up, you'll burn it down. This act of acceptance, this action of acknowledgement, is an amazing act of self-empowerment that actually facilitates positive change in your life.

What do I mean by that? The best examples in my life are my relationships with my family members. Those relationships are complex. But whose aren't, right? For me, it's always felt like my family dangled the carrot of connection in front of me, then yanked it away over and over again. This pattern has repeated itself over the years. So when does it become my responsibility to stop reaching for the carrot?

After *High on Arrival* came out—along with my truth about the abuse by my father, the drugs, the neglect, and the incest—my family relationships were strained. I would wake up every day thinking about what I could do to basically manipulate my family back into my life. What text can I send, what words can I use to show them that it's just me—to remind them that they love me?

It became an obsession, and it wasn't healthy. I had to surrender to what the relationships were in that moment instead of trying to make the relationships what I wanted them to be. This was a difficult process, but I realized I had worked through it after a family drama over the holidays.

Right now, my computer sits on the unopened box of a special gift I purchased for a family member's birthday shortly after the release of *High on Arrival*. Sadly, I've never been able to give this gift to its intended recipient because, although I'd initially been invited to the birthday party, I was uninvited later. Another family member was angered that I might attend, and I was told she was just not willing to forgive me yet. She wouldn't forgive *me*! For abuses perpetrated against me as a child, or for exposing those abuses perhaps. Others in my life, from my son to my ex-husband to my sponsor to my coworkers were horrified and furious about this excuse. I was too.

This situation repeated itself a few years later, almost identically. There was a time when I was devastated about being uninvited to family gatherings. I was furious and I was crushed. I wanted desperately to figure out a way to fix everyone's pain. To have them see me as valuable and worthy. But I believe the adage: doing the same thing over and over again and expecting different results is the definition of insanity. And I am not insane. So instead of having a knee-jerk reaction to these hurtful things, I pause when agitated. I call my sponsors and my trusted advisors and my friends. The outcome is better for everybody.

I've come to understand that some in my family have chosen to hold on to the pain and anger they felt when I came out with the truth about my dad. I understand that they're still caught in a textbook response of devaluing the victim and holding up the perpetrator. This is a common response within families when there has been abuse perpetrated by a family member.

And so I have had to surrender to what is. That means letting go of responsibility for how others choose to feel and act. I understand that I have no control over how my family individually or collectively feels; it's really not about me, and it's not mine to carry. I can't tell them to learn about abuse, I can't force them to come to terms with it, and I can't make them let go of the pain. These things are not within my power.

I've also had to accept that, of course, I'd be the target of negative reactions and feelings because I'm the one who wrote the book and told a truth no one wanted to hear. If you're trying to maintain some sort of facade so you can avoid pain, the last thing you want is for the facade to be demolished.

I had to get to a place where I was okay on my own. For a while it felt like I was under the bell jar. That I was singular and an island, alone and bereft.

Then, how beautiful, I started to see my life as it was and realized that, although I love these people, it was all right to let go. Surrender is about accepting that people have their own journey and process, and being okay with the outcome instead of trying to control it with a power I don't possess.

Let them wear their sweatshirts with kittens. And it's okay if I wear a sweatshirt with the three wise monkeys instead (with a fourth "feel no evil" monkey on it).

I had to learn to be comfortable with the idea that all I needed to be doing was my own thing, and that I would be around if and when any of the relationships reset. The interesting thing is, when they did begin to reset, I was able to see the dysfunctional parts of the family dynamic—in both mine and theirs. We each had some, like pretty much every family.

Distance and grace allowed me to see the desperation of the scene I was in. I realized that desperation doesn't always have to involve sticking a needle in my arm or a bottle down my throat. It can involve emotional needs and wants and validation that take an unhealthy turn, that create self-talk that says, *Maybe I don't have value or worth; maybe I'm not okay if I don't have someone else to help me define myself and to tell me I have value for just being me.* I had to back away from the incredible need to make them come back to me long enough to be able to see that, oh my god, it may be even better as it is. Oh my god, it may be even better without them.

In the end, distance and grace, given to me by the practice of acceptance and surrender, forced me to redefine myself, to value myself, and to see my own worth. Now, the truth is that little visits over the phone and maybe occasional visits in person are enough. And that's okay. It doesn't have to be more than what it simply is.

It may sound like it was easy, but it wasn't. I grieved, and even though I chose to let go in the end, I felt like I'd lost a limb. But it's okay to grieve the loss of things we can't change. When you get past the point of the grief, then you're able to create something even better—something more fulfilling and healthier.

Surrendering to an outcome and just trusting the process is really powerful. I'm thinking back to when I was with my mom at the Motion Picture Mothers luncheon (it's basically what it sounds like: an event for mothers of famous people, like Bruce Willis's mom and Tom Selleck's mom). So there I am with my mom, and all of a sudden a woman comes up to me and blurts out, "You're still working, right?" I knew what she meant: you're still an actress, aren't you? Instead of telling her, "No, I've given up the whole acting thing to pursue the exciting life of a ne'er-do-well traveling with a troupe of vagabonds," I thought, *No, Mack, she seems like a nice lady; just make regular conversation.* So I told her how I'd gone back to school and that I now work as a counselor in a substance-abuse treatment facility. I shared a little bit of my passion for what I do and for bringing awareness to the rise in substance abuse. The conversation ended with her saying, "Oh, well, that's nice," followed by an awkward silence. Maybe I should have led with the troupe of vagabonds instead?

A part of me wanted to follow after her to share with her how powerful it had been for me to surrender to passion instead of expectation. For me, the expectation—acting—wasn't the path forward anymore, even though it was what everyone, including myself, expected of me. Accepting that my passion for helping people and bringing awareness to the challenges of substance abuse was something worthwhile was a kind of surrender. I loved acting and I still do, but surrendering to a different path was one of the most radical things I've ever done. And man, am I thankful that I had the strength to let go of one dream to reach out for another.

Identifying the aspects of your life that are worth fighting for and the ones that are better to let go of is a difficult process but a necessary one. In the context of addiction, it's this: know when drugs and alcohol have beaten you. It's a horrifying reality to face, but it's absolutely essential to recovery.

I was in treatment in Antigua many years ago. It was a beautiful place by the beach, and I spent a lot of time down by the water. One night, my counselor gave me a quote by Chief Joseph of the Nez Perce. I took the quote outside with me in the middle of the night, and I read it under the light of the full moon: "Hear me, my chiefs! I am tired; my heart is sick and sad. From where the sun now stands, I will fight no more forever."[1] We might have been separated by decades and cultures and vastly different contexts, but the chief's words shook me to my core. I cried, and I surrendered. I said to myself, *I will fight no more forever*.

What was it that I was fighting? What was I giving up? Why was I giving it up? How would this move me forward? That's what surrender is—asking these hard questions and finding ways to move forward with the answers that come. What reality am I resisting, that I'm not willing to surrender to? It's not, "I give up," but rather "What is it that's holding me back?" I guarantee it's not your auntie's kitten sweatshirts. It's something inside of you, and thus, only you can make the choice to move forward. As the Serenity Prayer says (that's right kids, it's your old, slightly stale but still useful-as-hell friend the Serenity Prayer), "God grant me the serenity to accept the things I cannot change, courage to change the things I can, and wisdom to know the difference."[2]

ACCEPT THIS

The next time you think about something in your past that upsets you, ask yourself out loud (or write it down), "Right now, in this moment, can I change what happened back then?" Hint: the answer to that question is always, always, always going to be no.

Now, after you've asked yourself the question and given yourself the answer, say or write this: "Yes, it happened, and right now, in this moment, I'm okay. I accept this."

The next time something happens in your present that upsets you, put yourself through similar steps. Say or write, "I accept that this is happening to me right now." Next, ask yourself, "Right now, in this moment, can I change something about this situation? If so, what would that thing be?" Even if that thing is just to call a friend or sponsor, to take a walk to clear your mind, or to spend five minutes cuddling your dog, it's on you to take your acceptance one step further into action.

Choosing to accept is powerful. Choosing to act on that acceptance is revolutionary.

IT WORKS IF YOU WORK IT

Take out two sheets of paper. On one, write a list of things you truly have no control over (when the sun sets, your shoe size, your partner's snoring). On the other, write a list of things you can control (whether or not you watch the sunset, what type of shoes you buy, whether or not you sleep with earplugs). Destroy the first list as an act of letting go.

6

Stranger in a Strange Land

On identity

Find out who you are and do it on purpose.
—Dolly Parton

A while ago, when I was struggling with some issues, I was sitting in my living room and a bird smacked into the window. I jumped up and ran outside before I even knew what I was doing. The bird lay in the yard, stunned. I think it was a wren of some sort; it had beautiful brown speckling and a grey breast. I didn't want to leave it there because cats regularly patrolled the neighborhood, so I gently scooped it up, holding it snugly but gently in my hands. Its heart was beating a million miles a minute, but it stayed still. I could feel the softness of the feathers and how light those delicate, hollow bones really are.

I went and sat in the backyard, holding the bird in my cupped hands for thirty minutes, maybe a little more. I waited until I felt its wings give a small twitch, and then I slowly opened my hands. It rested there for just a couple minutes more before, in a sudden flurry, it flew away.

I continued to sit there for a few moments more, full of some feeling I couldn't name, before I slowly stood up and went back into the house.

Later that night, thinking on it, still trying to figure out the feeling I couldn't name, I realized I was humbled by how the bird felt as I held it, its fragility juxtaposed against the power in my hands. I was humbled that I had kept it safe, which made me want to cry.

The bird, I realized, was like the truest part of myself. If care and patience, gentleness and kindness helped the bird recover from its headlong flight into the window, then why not me? Why not you? That's how it was in early recovery for me—my sense of self felt so fragile, like the bird cupped in my hands.

Even when my addiction was active, I could feel myself there, like a trembling thing with a crazed heartbeat, because I was more interested in holding a needle or a drink than in being gentle with myself. I broke my own wings a couple of times, along with other delicate things.

One of the most messed-up things about addiction is that the damage you do is all you. You're not a different person when you're using, even though the addiction's driving; you're still a version of you. Those are *your* hands doing all of that harm to your sense of self; you simply do not have control over it. There are different concepts of what self is, but most agree the self is the essential nature that makes you unique and is responsible for your thoughts and actions. This does not mean that you have total control but that the self is liable or accountable for thoughts and actions. For the most part, when you are healthy, your sense of self is of a self that is unified.

Addiction fragments you into different pieces; your sense of self is supplanted by compulsive behaviors and the need to get your next fix. Your body is driven by it, as are your decisions and general thinking. Your spirit, for lack of a better word—that indelible thing that makes you *you*—sits vulnerable, shoved out of its nesting place by the inexplicable reality that you are doing this to yourself. And this dislocation of self causes the most caustic damage—the worst trauma that addiction delivers to our identity.

Most of the time, people think of trauma as an event, a sudden shock of some kind. But trauma can come from chronic stress and strain as well, and both can be applied to addiction in its different stages. Because of this, when we come into recovery, there's a feeling of being fragmented, compulsion having shoved our united sense of self out of the way. It can feel like being a stranger in strange skin— you are unrecognizable to yourself, and nothing feels like it fits.

When we think, *Oh my god, I've totally burned my life down. I have nothing. I feel like I'm nothing. Who is this person? I'm not this person*, it's hard to look at these thoughts, and it feels like shit when we do. When I look at clients at this stage, I see individuals who can't even see their own individuality. I see people who, on some level, think of themselves as just the drug or the drink: *I am heroin. I am vodka.* But from where I sit, I see individuals separate from their drugs and their drink. I see beautiful people who can't yet see their beauty. Perspective is everything, and all the beauty that is within them allows me to see my own. Soon, they'll see themselves as I see them.

Most of us have a hard time seeing our own beauty when we're struggling with reintegrating all of the pieces of ourselves because a lot of the processes in treatment focus on past behavior and negative consequences: whose hearts we broke, all the lies we told. It's easy to just see ugliness.

But even ugliness is beautiful in its own way. This is because the universe doesn't tolerate a lack of balance. The tide, it ebbs and flows. The sun rises and sets. The moon waxes and wanes. Balance.

When thinking about darkness and light, sadness and hope, I'm always reminded of a story from one of my times in treatment. We were doing "music therapy"—I'm using quotation marks here because, while I'm sure it worked great for some people, it drove me up the fucking wall. We'd sit around in a circle with handheld instruments and play along (badly) with records. It felt like the lamest thing in the entire world. So there I was, sitting in my long dress with my hair in a bun, shaking my maracas and mumbling "Raindrops keep fallin' on my head," and my monkey mind's chattering away, saying things like, *I've been onstage in front of 35,000 people. What am I doing?!* and *This is stupid!* But then the next song came on, and I was suddenly struck silent.

The song was the Prayer of Saint Francis set to music. Part of the prayer goes like this: "Lord, make me an instrument of thy peace. Where there is hatred, let me sow love; where there is injury, pardon; where there is doubt, faith; where there is despair, hope; where there is darkness, light; where there is sadness, joy." I was speechless. It was just so beautiful in what it was asking of me, of all of us. It brought me peace in a moment when I had none, and those simple yet profound words brought me balance.

When you're presented with examples of all of the negative shit that's happened in the past—all the discord and the mistakes and the pain—it can be really easy to lose your sense of identity along the way. When you feel yourself starting to slip-slide down into a pit of self-hatred and negative self-talk, fight to bring the good into focus. The things you're living for. The things you're working toward. Yes, you've probably done some things you're far from proud of. You may again. But that doesn't mean you aren't capable of reaching (or that you don't deserve to have) the good stuff on the other side too.

I was driving through Laurel Canyon one day, which is a place that's associated with a lot of memories for me, both good and bad. It's a place that I've traveled hundreds if not thousands of times. It's a place where I lived. It's also a place where my house burned down. It's a place that reminds me of both the positive (a sense of freedom) and the negative (late at night, driving loaded).

I'm sitting there on that drive one day, and the traffic is brutal. Terrible. I'm on my way back from an audition that I feel like I blew. I'm completely in the shit. The negative thoughts are swarming in. All of a sudden, I see my hands on the steering wheel, and I think, *I'm driving*. I think, *These are my hands. These hands have held a needle, and these hands soothed a baby. These are my hands.*

It was such a powerful moment that took me out of "future tripping," regret for the past, and sitting in traffic in a geographical location that holds great emotional power for me. I was able to re-enter my body in that moment. I was able to say, "These are mine. I own this." It brought me such peace and joy, this awareness that I could use my hands to destroy or I can use them to create. This was maybe twenty years ago, but even now, I'll look at my hands sometimes and remember that moment when I actually came to the realization that my hands had the power to build or to tear down.

As you focus on all that went wrong, remember all that went right too. When you're taking stock of when you were cruel, remember when you were kind. When you're listing all of your faults, list your good attributes too.

Remember the people who love you. Remember the creative spark of life that's within you.

As you struggle to reseat your sense of self, you're going to feel uncomfortable, and it's going to be really crappy, but breathe through it. Feeling uncomfortable and crappy is okay. Just *being* what you're really feeling is okay.

If you ask yourself the question, *Who will I be when I'm sober?* When you answer, be fearless.

Are you a total metalhead who was a heroin addict? You can still be a total metalhead and not be a heroin addict while you're doing it. Let your freak flag fly, however it flies. Be who you are, but be sober.

If I were to fearlessly answer the question *Who am I?* my answer would go like this: I'm playful. I'm silly. I'm really smart. I'm a good friend. I'm a fucking awesome mom. I'm compassionate. I'm an empath. I'm an intuitive person. I'm an introverted extrovert.

I have a great love of old, beautiful things. I like to have a place to go. I like to be expected somewhere. I like to have a task at hand. I like to have purpose. I like going to bed at night and reading books and watching TV, and I like talking to my dogs. I need to be on my own in order to recharge. I love junk food—Twizzlers and Laffy Taffy and chocolate (which, let's be real, isn't junk—it's manna from heaven!).

I'm a naturally cheerful person, a happy monkey—I was born that way. I'm built that way. I'm resilient. No matter what's going on, I can do whatever needs to be done.

I'm a super-high-energy person. I love to twist my double-jointed limbs up into weird tangles—I'll be facilitating a group, and I'll look down and think, *Oh my god, my shoes are off, and I'm twisted up like some sort of human pretzel in front of twenty clients!* That's better than forcing myself to sit normally. I wouldn't be living my authentic self if I did. I don't pretend to be some sort of authority figure; I try to keep things real.

There are things about you that are just the way you are.

All of that makes you who you are.

This is not to say that I'm all types of awesome all of the time. I can be ego driven, intolerant, impatient, unkind, defiant, stubborn, and a downright shit. I can get emotionally down and uncertain. I worry and get fearful. I sometimes feel put upon, and I sometimes drag my feet on decisions.

While I was using, I was still that naturally happy person, only in a messed-up, distorted way. "Let's all shoot some coke! This is beautiful! We are living outside the confines of society; isn't this awesome?" It's a sick twist on how the disease acts on your thought process, and it's one of the things that keeps people from getting well because the dysfunction takes what's good about yourself and twists it to its advantage.

Even though the disease takes your identity and sense of self and mangles it to suit its own purposes, that doesn't mean your identity is irrevocably lost. Be fearless in the face of these challenges. Don't distance yourself from the good or the bad; this is about knitting yourself back together, not pulling yourself further apart. When you see things you like, mindfully encourage these things in yourself. When you see things you don't like, mindfully work at shifting these aspects of yourself (remember to practice mindfulness in all things, like we talked about back in chapter 3). Take self-inventory on a regular basis and work to make it right if you've done wrong. These are the things you do to find yourself again.

COMPASSION MATTERS

Perfection is not required for recovery, but self-honesty is. And so is self-compassion.

Be kind.

Be patient.

Be forgiving.

Be tough on yourself.

Be humble.

Be hopeful.

Ask questions.

Give of yourself.

Ask for help.

Accept help.

Listen for wisdom.

Let yourself love.

And let yourself be loved.

IT WORKS IF YOU WORK IT

Are there aspects of your personality that you like but lost while you were in active addiction? Write a love note to yourself praising those traits. Put it in an envelope, address it to yourself, and affix a stamp. Give the letter to someone you trust. Ask them to mail it to you the next time they see you getting down on yourself.

Life Is Messy

On choice, responsibility, and consequence

In the long run, we shape our lives, and we shape ourselves.
The process never ends until we die. And the choices we make
are ultimately our own responsibility.

— Eleanor Roosevelt

I have only acted in color, as black and white began being phased out from movies and television almost two decades before my first role. It's interesting that, as color slowly replaced black and white, characters in the movies and on TV shows seemed to better reflect real lives in the real world. Shows like *All in the Family* and my own show, *One Day at a Time*, were driven by family dynamics and daily struggles. The world was no longer portrayed in a limiting black and white; it was presented in a spectrum, complex and multilayered, making for better, more compelling storylines for both movies and television.

It's funny that in real life, we have a tendency to want black-and-white certainties. Clear-cut lines between cause and effect. But that's not always the way it works. We want to have formulas that give precise answers and guaranteed predictions. We want to find the choice that caused a particular outcome.

If only it were that easy. Life is full of layers of choices and layers of results. I like to think about it as painting with watercolor, everything flowing into everything else with translucent, delicate layers. Everyone's life is bumping, like watercolors, against everyone else's lives, because, like it or not, we're all a part of an unbelievably large canvas, each of us adding our own bit to the larger picture. Think about your choices as the colors you add or don't add. You are responsible for what they do on the canvas, whether they create a brilliant hue that clarifies a bit of the picture or whether they muddy it. The other colors that are being painted by someone who is not you—the way the water already on the paper makes the colors run, and the aims and visions of the other painters—turns the endeavor into a communal effort. Are you working well in the painting? Are you putting a splash of blue next to chartreuse, or are you making things clash? Are you mindfully trying to be a part of things or are you setting yourself apart from them, the way you did in your active addiction? On this canvas called life, it's all about the choices we make and then the results of those choices. Did I make something better or worse? I'm responsible for whatever those choices are and for whatever I do. I'm accountable for my actions and my words, good or bad. And the consequences are mine as well, good or bad.

When talking with my clients about choice, I will often give them this metaphor: Think of choices like a beautiful tree—a very old tree—with all kinds of branches that intersect with each other. Imagine yourself standing at the base of this beautiful old tree. As you climb up toward recovery and wellness, each branch represents a different path you can take. Will you reach for the branches that don't look so sturdy, or will you go for the ones that look stronger and that are closer to the next branch you need to aim for to get to the top? The key is to evaluate—to determine whether going out on a particular branch will leave you hung out to dry or whether you'll be able to reach the next branch to your next choice from there. You can be like a crazy monkey, jumping from branch to branch until you land on one that breaks or leaves you with nowhere to go; or you can mindfully choose a path. What's great about taking the mindful route is that you can see that choosing a particular path doesn't prevent you from going off in a new direction later. You can see that your current path intersects with other options ahead.

The choice tree holds two possibilities: (1) it can be a wonderful thing full of branches and options that lead you onward to the next branch that takes you ever higher, or (2) it can be a dangerous place full of dead branches that go nowhere. You get to choose which it will be for you.

Here's the truth: you won't get very far without some planning. It is essential to plot your path.

With life as complex as it is, it's important to figure out strategies for how we go about dealing with all of it—and without drugs or alcohol. Most people do not consciously create a strategy for decision making. They do it on the go, based off of experience, the situation at hand, and what they've been taught. An addict can't and shouldn't rely on their automatic decision-making ability; their addiction makes that ability unreliable at best because it has its own agenda to get high or drunk. So give yourself a blueprint for making decisions. (And understanding that even deciding to do nothing is a choice.) Before I do something I'm not sure of, I ask for help—I call my sponsor or my best friend. Asking for help is a great strategy. My trusted advisers ask me some basic questions:

- Will this harm anyone (myself included)?
- Is it respectful of myself and others?
- Will it make things better or worse?
- Is it kind?
- Is it necessary?
- Is it true?

After I've made my call, I have a few additional questions:

- Have I acted with love?
- Am I being fair?

You don't have to have the same strategy, but you do need a strategy—some kind of criteria that allows you to consistently make the safest and healthiest choices you are able to make. Once you get it, stick to it, work it, be fierce and stubborn about it. Because it's hard to hold on to a strategy that moves you away from your addictive reward system.

After the decision comes the responsibility and the consequence. We often come at taking responsibility for our actions from a moralistic or judgmental place—was this good or bad?—when internally we really mean am *I* good or bad because I made this good or bad decision or did this good or bad thing?

If it's a good thing, we are usually pretty okay with taking responsibility for it and accepting the consequences. If it's a bad thing, well that's a shitty feeling, and why deal with it when it can be ignored or smothered by shooting up or drinking?

Bad decisions humble us and cause us pain. Pain leaves a memory imprint in the brain so that we have it to reference if a similar situation arises, so we don't do it again. When you try to circumvent that pain with drugs or alcohol, you mess it up. You make a mistake and then you repeat it. Even worse, because you get high to avoid the whole thing, you're basically giving yourself a reward for bad choices. Talk about messed up.

How do we navigate that? Well, first, don't put it into a place of moralistic judgment so quickly. Let it be what it is. Acknowledge to yourself that you made the decision and that the consequences are happening (remember acceptance and surrender?). Those are facts. Once you have that, you can then look at whether you have made a choice that doesn't—in some way, shape, or form—betray who you are at your core.

That's the hardest thing, I think—to know that you are responsible for your own wounding. We so very often equate who we are with what we do that when we do ourselves wrong, we start to think we deserve it. No, you don't deserve to forever beat yourself up for making bad choices. Think of it as accountability: you are obligated to get up and change so you do not make the same bad choices again. Chalk it up to experience and raise the bar.

This can be hard—majorly hard. The getting back up part is an epic thing on its own but so is making better choices and taking responsibility; it's just not as showy.

With all of this grown-up decision making comes taking reasonable responsibility and accepting the consequences. First, taking responsibility is a powerful act. It is one that offers self-respect. It says, "I'm strong enough to handle the consequences." It's the most powerful form of personal choice and action—right up there with making a decision. It is one of the things in life that you have complete control over.

Taking responsibility is also something that is trustworthy; it sets up reciprocity and shows wisdom. It helps people start to see *you* and not the addict.

I want to stop for a second and talk about decisions that are made and actions that are taken when the responsibility does not lie with you—like when someone is being abused, whether as a child or as an adult. I was groomed by my father, and the outcome of that was that he drugged me and he had sex with me. When there's abuse of power involved, responsibility *always* lies with the abuser.

So what is the strategy for taking responsibility when the responsibility is yours to take?

You can start by acknowledging that life is freaking complex. That it's not going to be these clear, neat scenarios. Responsibility and consequence—choices—they're a part of a complex relational thing, which can be super frustrating when you're trying to establish what the hell is going on during your recovery.

You can't have a conversation about responsibility without also having a conversation about support. That goes back to speaking about having help as you go through your process of understanding what's yours to carry and what isn't. When you're trying to fix something that's broken, you need others who have experience, who have perspective, who have been there, who can act as sounding boards, and whose lives can be great examples of what can happen as you work the process of recovery.

My own experience is deeply rooted with having support systems and started with my time going to 12-step meetings, where having a sponsor and going to meetings were core aspects of the program.

Then support came through doing clinical work. I cannot stress enough the amazing amount of good that having people around you can bring. They are there for the good, the bad, and everything in between. They offer everything from sound advice to practical solutions to just being an open ear when you need it.

It's important to note that not all addiction counselors are in recovery themselves. Some of them are; but even if they're not in recovery, they still have that breadth of knowledge to share and from which you can learn some truly life-changing stuff. Also, there is a big difference between a sponsor and a counselor. A sponsor's job is to walk you through the 12-step process. To be there when you need support—a hand to help you when you fall down. Your relationship with your counselor is more actively therapeutic. With the consistency of seeing a counselor, you can delve into the underlying issues behind your addiction and plan for the future. Both of these kinds of people in your life can offer you a picture of what recovery can look like. Not what recovery will always look like but what it can look like if you're willing to do the work.

When you're deep in your addiction, it's hard for negative consequences to reach you. *My life's gone to complete shit? Hey, at least I can still get high.* When you're in this frame of mind, seeing what life could be like in recovery through the example of your sponsor or counselor can be super powerful.

Learning to see the complexity of your life as being beautiful is freeing. It's freeing to know that you are more than one thing at a time; that you have layers to yourself; that you can say, "I can be happy, and right underneath that, I can be sad," and know that both things are okay and both things are true. We're allowed to be complex. We're allowed to have it be messy. Life is a hot, unraveled-yarn mess. And the mess usually has consequences.

Consequence—the result of a decision, of a choice, of an action. The consequence of a choice can be both good and bad. But for you, an addict, deciding to take drugs or to drink will always end in bad consequences. *Always.* The ramifications for your brain, your spirit, and your life are all negative. And you always have to live with them. Always. Brutal.

There are no side roads you can take to avoid the consequences, mostly because the consequence of an action is the destination. It may take you a while to get there, but you *will* get there. Just know that if you decide to try and avoid the destination for as long as possible, you will almost certainly create more chaos along the way and have more consequences to deal with when you arrive. So, that being the case, the best course of action is to own and accept the consequences and make a beginning. Do not linger at the rest stop. Does this sound like fun? Of course it doesn't, but do it anyway.

Why? Because waiting to deal with consequences is emotionally crushing. Putting off the inevitable only makes the inevitable more difficult to face. The dread of what might happen takes up residence in our thoughts and our bodies, and pushes everything else away. You live waiting for the shoe to drop, even if you try to fill up your life with other distractions (like drugs or alcohol or sex or shopping).

It's scary, owning and accepting a bad consequence. You might end up with people being angry and hurt or in jail, or you might lose something like your license or, far worse, your child. But here's the deal: these things might happen whether you've owned the consequence or not. I lost jobs several times as a consequence of my drug use, each time without owning it. When I was fired from *One Day at a Time* the second time, I thought, *Oh well, I'm a big star. Someone else will want me.* That did not happen. And I pretended I didn't care, didn't need to change anything. The difference between owning a consequence and having a consequence roll out just because that's the nature of the beast is the difference between actively working to change and passively sitting there hoping change happens. *Active* versus *passive*.

You have several choices as you consider the consequences. You can carefully look at what got you into this mess, learn from it, and move on. Or you can judge and berate yourself, and stay in a place of self-loathing. It seems like a no-brainer, but we all have times when we don't learn from our shit and times when we get so caught up in how bad we fucked up that it's hard to get past it. Still, even when you've completely demolished your life, you've got to move on from it. This is key. Do not dwell. You did a messed-up thing, and now it's time to face the music—and sooner rather than later. Call on your mindfulness to recognize that if you don't consciously break this cycle, you're going to repeat and repeat and repeat it. Your addiction is lying to you when it says, "Hey, that wasn't so bad, right?" It *was* that bad, trust me. Call on your support network, and be brave.

Use your blueprint moving forward to make sure your decisions are ones you won't regret down the line. Think through which colors you are going to add to the canvas. Aim to make your contribution a vibrant, thoughtful one. Paint your choices so that you offer help and hope to yourself and others. And if you sometimes mix murky colors or bleed messily into other spots, then work to balance that with your next stroke.

Informed decision making is a skill—one you have to practice even if you aren't an addict. We don't really think often about long-term consequences. People are just trying to live the life they have right now, so they have a tendency to be pretty shortsighted. But as we grow—and grow up—it becomes pretty clear that we have to make some changes.

When looking at a decision, you can also ask yourself, *What are the results I want to see? Are they short term or long term? How will they change me?*

Recovery (and the strategies and processes for getting there) involves planning for a combination of short-term and long-term results. While you're working on this stuff right now, there are some results you will see right away. But just as often, there are results you won't see until much, much later. Make patience a part of your process. And if you think you don't have any patience to spare, then look to hope—that steadfast partner that is kind of like patience with a little bit of love mixed in.

STAGES OF CHANGE

When you're thinking about choices, responsibility, and consequences, it can be really helpful to view these things through a broader lens of where you are on the path to recovery. Psychologists Carlo C. DiClemente and J. O. Prochaska, cocreators of the transtheoretical model of behavioral change, came up with something called the stages of change model. It's a five-stage model to help people who work with addicts understand how the process of change works for an addict, and how to help their clients effect positive and lasting change in their lives.[1] It goes like this:

1. Precontemplation—This is before you even realize that you have a problem or are even giving any thought to changing your behavior. At this stage, you can be reluctant to recognize that you have a problem, rebellious/resistant to the idea of changing your life and habits, resigned to the seeming inevitability of your addiction, or overly rational about your addiction. Denial ain't just a river in Egypt. ("There's nothing wrong, and here's why!")

2. Contemplation—This is when you start to entertain the possibility that you've got a major problem that you're probably going to

have to deal with. This stage hurts, but it's important. You haven't yet made the decision to change your behavior, but you're giving it some thought.

3. Preparation—It's go time, my friends. When in the preparation stage, you've made a commitment to taking action, which can be even scarier than thinking about taking action. This is when shit gets serious.

4. Action—Now it's time to follow through. *Gulp*. This stage is all about taking your plan of action and putting it in motion. This is usually when counseling comes in: checking in to a center, going to a 12-step program, seeing a therapist. This stage is also about making a formal commitment by announcing to the people in your life that you're serious about kicking your addiction out the door and never opening that door again. And you vow that you'll do whatever it takes to recover. This is when you prove that sucker wrong—that you can beat addiction and will.

5. Maintenance—This is when the real work begins. Taking action is great, but maintaining that action is another battle entirely. You're forming new behaviors, you're creating new habits, you're changing your relationships for the better. The possibility of relapse is always real, but this is also the stage in which you arm yourself with a set of skills that will make you less likely to slide back into places you've determined that you're going to leave behind.

Phew! A lot to take in, right? Don't worry, this is just a primer. I highly encourage you to talk to your counselor or sponsor about the stages of change. It helped me to recognize where I was in the process.

While you go through these stages, you will likely work on some specific things with your recovery team. Stuff like fully acknowledging the problem and getting really honest about whether or not you're effectively self-regulating your feelings, thoughts, and behaviors. (Spoiler alert: if you're using, you're not self-regulating).

You'll work on getting a grip on the risk versus the reward of continuing to use and, I hope and pray, you'll realize that the risks of using far exceed the rewards. You'll learn about setting goals and priorities, and you'll put together a plan to help you walk through the process of changing your unhealthy behaviors in a way that is safe and workable. And you just might save your own life. The end goal is to integrate your new way of being into your regular life so that it is just that: regular.

IT WORKS IF YOU WORK IT

Using the blueprint for decision making (on page 77) as a reference point, develop your own blueprint. This is something you might want to work on with a sponsor or counselor.

Dead-End Streets Have Sidewalks Too

On shame, guilt, and regret

We don't see things as they are, we see them as we are.

—**Anaïs Nin**

Shame, guilt, and regret: an addict's emotional trifecta of shitty ways to feel. These are the three dark places you go to when you look at something really bad in your life that you did. When you're spending time in these dark places, it feels like there's no way out. Sometimes we go there without realizing it, and sometimes we go there on purpose. Sometimes we go there purposely to continue the process of our self-flagellation. It's like when you listen to a sad song to make yourself cry—it's dangerous territory. It's a dead end after a wrong turn, with three houses of horror to hang out in. Much like the Hotel California, if you take up residence in any of these houses, you're going to have a hard time leaving.

If you're living in your house of shame, you'll still end up in painful conversations with regret and guilt. Guilt and regret follow closely behind shame. Shame is a feeling of distress or humiliation for who you are. Guilt is feeling culpable for what you do. Regret is feeling sad and disappointed that something happened, particularly when your own decisions brought you to the thing you're regretting.

I grew up in a cul-de-sac, which is like a cousin to the dead-end street, the difference being that a cul-de-sac is built so that you can circle your way back out. Mine had a handy little walkway that took you to the street behind the cul-de-sac. A walkway of possibility. On the street where shame, guilt, and regret exist, there are also walkways of possibility. But before we talk about how to access them, we have to talk about how each of these haunted houses work, and how they relate to addiction and recovery. Let's start with shame.

Feeling shame is one of the biggest roadblocks to recovery and is one of the biggest culprits in relapse.[1] It's perhaps as powerful as it is because it has such a physicality to it—there is a flush of heat that washes across our bodies, and we turn or hide our faces away when we feel it. We tremble and collapse into ourselves when we're feeling it very deeply.

Shame freezes a moment in time when we believe we were at our worst and holds it up like a mirror so the worst version of ourselves is what we see. Shame is the state we put ourselves into when we feel that we have committed a deep violation of who we are supposed to be in our own eyes and in the eyes of society.

Out of these three feelings, shame is the most destructive because it is connected to our core selves. Shame is the gap between who we perceive ourselves to be and what we know to be right. We feel shame when we fail to meet that interior moral standard. It's a self-imposed judgment that measures the gap. The greater the distance, the more unworthy we deem ourselves to be.

If it's within a normal range, shame is a deterrent. Guilt and regret are also meant to deter, but because of the peculiar twist of addiction, these deterrents rarely deter.

No one wants to feel shame, so we strive to be true to our moral core, to meet our internal as well as societal standards. It is when we can't recover from the feeling of unworthiness that can accompany shame that we start having a problem. And for addicts, who have a long list of all the ways they did not live up to internal and societal standards, shame can become a self-blame narrative that cycles in on itself until, after a while, the shame stops being about a specific moment of failure or humiliation and starts being about who the whole person is all of the time.

It's an internal dialogue that starts with, "I'm a failure," and goes straight to, "No one would love me if they really knew me; they would see I am horrible and unworthy." The fact that you feel that way becomes its own shame as well.

It also becomes a secret. Like the little kid who puts a blanket over his head and believes he's invisible. If I just don't look at it, it can't see me. If I can just escape from this situation (take a hit, down this beer or five), then it'll go away. The cycle of shame exists because you're not looking at it; it grows and builds and builds and builds.

How do we break that shame cycle? We separate shame from guilt. Go ahead and feel guilty about being an asshole if you've been an asshole. But don't feel like that moment of being an asshole is the entirety of who you are (unless you're a perpetual asshole, but that's a conversation for another time). In other words, start assessing your shame and look for the moments where the shame is based on an action you took. And then remind yourself that you are not that choice. You are the person behind that choice. These are two different things.

In her beautiful song "I Am Light," India Arie insists she is not defined by the actions of her family, or her own mistakes or pain. She sings, "I am not the pieces of the brokenness inside. I am light, I am light."

It brings me to tears every time I hear it because it captures the essence of this conversation about shame.

How to break the cycle? Begin to take a serious look at the standard to which you are holding yourself; specifically, the one that you feel you are failing to meet. What I found when I did this work for myself was that my expectations of what it takes for me to be worthy were crazy. No one could actually meet them all of the time. Some of them were just outright not doable. I mean, some of my expectation was that I was supposed to always be happy. Never sad. I was a failure if I was sad. No one can be happy all of the time, but I somehow thought I should be. So figure out your true standards—the reasonable standards—that are reachable for you.

Talk about it with someone you trust. Or say it out loud. Or write it down. Shame is strongest when we don't speak about it. Bring it into the open. Say, "I feel ashamed." Say why you feel ashamed. Listen to it. Let it be what it is. Then take a deep breath and release it. Give yourself the same compassion you would give someone else who was being eaten up by unreasonable shame. Tell yourself, *I am worthy even if I fail, even if I make a mistake.*

I had this sponsor who was my trusted advisor. She was a dedicated sweatshirt wearer; and she had the most amazing bright-red helmet hair, wore pink lipstick and elastic-waisted polyester pants, and lived in a trailer. I remember thinking, *Oh god, how can I tell her all the shameful things that I feel guilty about and that I regret?* Then I figured, *I just have to do it because I'm desperate.* That desperation was a kind of gift in its own way because it gave me the shove I needed to take that next step. In that moment, I wanted to be like her. Not that I wanted to wear the sweatshirts and rock the helmet hair, but I wanted to be happy and comfortable in the here and now without a drink and a drug.

I was sitting there on the porch of her trailer under a striped umbrella. I started reading her my fourth step, which is a moral inventory, and she said, "Honey, what you see here is not what was going on thirty years ago, when I was still out there." She basically said, "I can one-up you."

This was my aha moment of connection: I'm not alone. I can reveal myself, and I want to connect instead of hide. One moment of connection can open up a world of awareness. Connection is the antidote for shame, and shame can be a pride-in-reverse kind of thing—I'm the worst of the worst; no one could be worse than me. But then you find out that, no, other people have felt that too. That's when the shame starts to take the backseat instead of the front.

I remember thinking, *I'm so fundamentally broken at my core that if I tell this woman the horrors of what I've done, she is going to explode and be reduced to a little pink pile of powder on that lawn chair right before my eyes.* But I needed to tell her. I needed to expose my shame to the sunlight and let the rays sizzle that fucker to death like a vampire.

After I'd finished my litany of how horrible I was, she cackled and said, "Oh, honey, you think you're bad?" and proceeded to tell me her own story. It made me feel like it was okay to be me—like it was okay to have survived. Instead of shunning me or judging me, she accepted me and shared a part of herself with me as well. We were able to laugh and cry, and then we were able to move on.

Let's take on guilt next. I want to distinguish guilt from shame. Guilt is when you look back and you say, *Oh my god, I pawned my mother's diamonds* or *Oh my god, I lied to my family so that I could go get high*. These thoughts feed into the shame of *I am bad, I am broken*, but are not in and of themselves thoughts of shame. The goal here is to understand and believe that you are not the shameful things that you've done.

A therapist I once had said something along these lines that was very powerful: "You feel shame for all these things that you believe you are. You feel guilt for all these things that you've done. But let me ask you, from your point of view on this day that we're living now, would you do those things now?"

Mind blown—just like that! *My god, no, I wouldn't ever do them now!* This realization gave me the opportunity to separate, if you will, my behavior in active addiction from my true self in recovery. A simple question: would I do that now? Unequivocally, absolutely, fuck no. When you frame it like that, the distinction becomes clear.

That question gives me an opportunity to look at the power of drugs and alcohol and then the power of compassion and love. I have enough compassion for myself and love for myself to admit to myself that I would never, *ever* have done those things had I not been in that state. That's not giving me a pass; it's balancing things out.

One thing that can fuck up this balance is regret. Let me start by saying how lame and, ultimately, useless regret is. This sounds harsh, but bear with me.

When Shane was around nine years old, we were late to his dentist appointment one day. He was fussing and pulling away from me in the parking lot, and I yanked on his arm too hard. That action of mine has bothered me for fifteen years, but when I asked Shane about it, he told me, "Mom, I don't even know what you're talking about. I don't remember that." It didn't register for him but left a huge mark on me—a mark that said I must be a bad parent, I must have scarred my child for life, I must be a terrible human being.

I still wish I hadn't gotten so fed up and yanked on my son's arm that day, but the act of regretting snowballed into guilt and then into a lasting shame that, ultimately, has done me no good.

In a way, regret is like wishful thinking. It's not attached to any forward motion or positive action. Yes, you can and should examine your past behaviors in order to make positive change in your present, but what good is looking backward going to do if you end up just wishing and wishing you'd done things differently? You can't change the past. Don't let yourself get stuck in that part of the cycle.

I can say to myself that I regret leaving the house with a bunch of drugs in my pocket and getting arrested. I wish that hadn't happened. But if everything that happened to me hadn't happened, I'd be dead. Unequivocally, I wouldn't be here. Change any one thing from my past, and it upsets the whole kit and caboodle.

If you were actually to physically create a timeline where certain past events never happened, you might not be the person you are now. Maybe the thing you're busy regretting is the one integral moment that needed to occur for your personal journey or growth.

Regret is a useless emotion—a useless mind-set—because you can't change the thing you regret. You can wish it never happened, but you can't change it. It's done, past, over with. The thing with regret is that it's easy to fall into it—to move in and stay steeped in it. I regret a thousand things, but I don't allow myself to live there.

For all their negativity, shame, guilt, and regret can be teachers and motivators. One of the most profound lessons I've ever learned from them (and am still learning) is that I'm human and, therefore, not perfect. I'm completely unable to be what someone else wants me to be; I'm only able to be who I am. And there is no shame, no guilt, and no regret to be found in that truth.

Shame, guilt, and regret can be teachers so long as you don't take up residence with them. Don't hang out at that nasty block party for too long or else that will become your permanent home. It's tempting to use our sense of shame, guilt, and regret to punish ourselves by dwelling in the horrible despair they bring us, but that's not where the path forward lies.

CHOOSING YOUR HOME

You choose the house you're going to live in. You furnish it. You choose whom to invite inside. Are you going to live alongside the shitty roommates of guilt, shame, and regret? Not if you have anything to say about it.

When you're buying a house, you do your research, you see many different houses before you decide, and then, after some deliberation, you pick the one for you. My son and I picked our house together. I wanted it to be *our* home, not just mine. It's a great memory, us sharing that choice.

In the same way that we pick physical housing to live in, everyone gets to choose their own interior home, the emotional housing they live in. Different things will influence your choice of home and its decor. You may choose to include others' feelings in your decor, or it may be all you. The important idea to hold on to no matter who or what you consider in your decision is that the house is yours.

Your home is yours to leave as is, to remodel at will, to redecorate, or to tear down. You get to choose. Choose wisely.

IT WORKS IF YOU WORK IT

Guilt and shame are difficult to distinguish from one another. We can spot shame because it usually starts with an *I am* statement: "I am a bad person because I did a bad thing." The next time you catch yourself engaging in shameful self-talk due to past actions, directly confront your thinking by stopping and asking the question, "Would I do this now?" And I would wager that your answer would be a distinctive no, stopping the shame spiral before it begins.

Do Better

On forgiveness and esteem

And to make an end is to make a beginning.
—T. S. Eliot

I was on the phone with a close friend—one of those friends that you count as family—when it happened. She was remembering something from years before, and in that memory, was a small bit about a lie I'd told her. My lie had left her in a tight situation, and she had to jump through some hoops to get out of it. I could feel myself tensing up, cringing a little bit more as the story went on.

As she continued to talk about what had happened and I continued to squirm with discomfort, I realized that her point wasn't about the fact that I had put her in a tough position; she was really talking about how she had solved the problem. And she was telling me about it with a "yay, I'm that awesome" tone. It dawned on me that (a) she had forgiven me, (b) it wasn't always about me, and (c) I hadn't really forgiven myself for my part in that long-ago drama.

I can tell you, being an addict myself, that most addicts are egomaniacs with inferiority complexes: "I'm fucking awesome! But I'm also a piece of shit." We live on two opposite ends of a spectrum. Usually, when we're having our piece-of-shit moments, we feel like we should be asking for forgiveness from somebody for the shit we've put people in our lives through. We often forget that, sometimes, the person we need to forgive the most is ourself.

It's tricky, this forgiveness thing. When we talk about forgiveness, we're usually talking about it in one of three ways:

Please forgive me.
I forgive you.
I forgive myself.

All three are tied up in some way, shape, or form with self-esteem and esteem in general. For an addict, the dialogue of forgiveness, both the external and internal, plays a large role in reestablishing that esteem.

It's a lifelong process, finding this place inside yourself that is more reality based. A place from which you can say, "Yeah, that happened, I did that; but I would never do it now." For example, shooting coke all through my pregnancy and knowing that my actions were completely insane. It was like flipping off God and the beautiful child that He had chosen to give me. I would never do that now. Should I apologize to Shane every day for shooting coke while I was pregnant? No. Is that appropriate? Absolutely not. Does he know about it? Yes. So how do I deal with that? I just do better. That's all anyone can do: just do better. Acknowledge, discuss, move on. Then you use love to heal that place—that broken place.

Self-forgiveness can be crazy tricky. What do you forgive yourself for? For the harm you've done to yourself seems the obvious answer. But to what level do we go? I had to forgive myself for using while pregnant and for using again after ten years of being clean. I betrayed some of my core beliefs and pretty much ravaged my self-trust. Forgiving myself took some doing.

But at a certain point, I realized I had been forgiving myself for stuff that wasn't mine. One time, I was in my car, listening to the oldies station, when a song from The Mamas and the Papas came on. I said, "Hi, Dad," out loud. I immediately cringed and started to analyze the moment: *What does this mean? Is this bad? Does my acknowledging him mean I've betrayed my truth that he hurt me?* It wasn't until later, when I had a little more wisdom on board, that I could see it in a different way and find my forgiveness in this context. First, not everything has to have a deeper meaning and connection. Second, he was my dad and I loved him, so of course, I'd say hi. That was all I needed to carry away from that moment.

I've had lots of little moments when I've overanalyzed things. When I catch myself, I've learned to give myself a wry inner smile and say, *Yep, that's me, and that's okay*. When I don't catch myself, I find myself going down a rabbit hole of regret and incrimination before I remember to redirect myself to where I'm at in my life now—to refocus on the present. At a certain point, you realize you've done the deed—you're practicing self-forgiveness. It's either that or choosing to be perpetually stuck in the past. And you know it's better to be in the now.

My son and I have an amazing relationship, but he's extremely opinionated and literal and adamant. I'm not. I'm flighty and wildly fluctuating, and I'm also a born-and-bred optimist. He, on the other hand, is a pessimist. When you have two people like that living in a house together, some conflicts are bound to rise up. Sometimes, I put on my big-girl pants and suck it up because he needs to have his say, and other times, I roll my eyes and think, *Oh boy, here we go again*. What I've learned to do is consciously see him as beautiful and magical and perfectly himself even though we're very different people. That in itself is a form of forgiveness. It's not capital *F* forgiveness but little *f* forgiveness. It's a happy capitulation and acceptance—a surrender.

In a way, forgiveness can become almost a lifestyle, or maybe an everyday philosophy. It's moving through life understanding that a person's going to make mistakes—that *you're* going to make mistakes. For the most part, no one goes into life with the intention to cause damage. The damage is usually inadvertent and unforeseen— not intentional at all. Think about how often people are surprised when you tell them that they've hurt your feelings. They have no idea. So a philosophy of forgiveness might include a general blanket of forgiveness for the little crappity-crap; for the stuff that's not aimed at anyone; for the shit that's just there.

Do I think that my father held me in his arms when I was a baby and thought, *I'm going to abuse my daughter some day*? No. I think that a toxic combination of chance and circumstance and drugs and alcohol morphed into something dark and ugly. I don't think that what he did was his intention; I don't think that he planned to do what he did, and I think that I can see him as a deeply flawed human being in light of all this. I can forgive that flaw. It doesn't mean that I can accept the act—or that I should—but that I can see it for what it wasn't as well as what it was. Forgiveness is complex.

During the final stage of writing this book, my mom passed away. She fell on a Wednesday and died on Friday night. All day long at the hospital, she was saying, "This is bullshit. This is bullshit." And I would say, "Yeah, Mom, you're right. This is bullshit."

My mother had dementia—my mother who was Robert McNamara's personal secretary at the Pentagon, my mother who danced in the Vienna ballet—my brilliant mother. I sometimes still had to force myself to visit her at her assisted-living home. If I wasn't there to hug her, then no one was going to hug her. When I think about it, it still feels agonizing. But then I'd see her, and she would be just so happy in her little world. Her world had gotten extremely small, but she just wanted to be loved.

Sometimes I had thoughts like, *Oh god, my poor mommy*, but then I'd see her and know that all of my angst was about me. She didn't see herself as this poor woman who used to be all of those things. I had to remind myself that the situation was hard. That I was going to have a lot of feelings about it. I was going to think a lot of thoughts about it. Was it appropriate for me to say to my eighty-year-old mother who had dementia and wore diapers, "I'm so disappointed that you're not who you used to be. I need my mommy"? No, saying that wasn't going to help. It was not going to make anything better even though it might have given me a moment of relief to have it out in the open. And if I would have said the words, I would have felt miserable the minute after. This is something for which I must find the power within me to self-forgive, because it's okay to be scared. It's okay to want to run away. It's okay to feel helpless.

These kinds of thoughts occur in all of us who are dealing with something difficult. You have a child, and your child is pushing your very last button. In your mind's eye, you can see yourself lashing out.

Basically throwing a tantrum at the kid throwing a tantrum. Do you do it? No.

We think that having these thoughts makes us abnormal or bad, when they're actually just thoughts. That's a part of the human condition. Recognizing that is a form of self-forgiveness—not as an excuse to act on them but, rather, as a way of connecting with your humanity. I remind myself that it was human to feel a lot of feelings about my relationship with my mother, and I remind myself that it could not get better because of the downward progression of dementia.

On the last day of my mom's life, I was playing some music for her. My brother was out of the room, so it was just the two of us and a nurse in the room. I put on "Do You Know the Way to San Jose" (my mom loved Burt Bacharach). She was completely loaded on morphine, and it was her last real interaction with anybody. She was lying on the bed, waving her little hand. Her cat, Bubbles, jumped up next to her, and my mom said, "You know, I never liked that fucking cat." She was wasted. "That cat's a bitch. The one thing I like about that cat—that cat knows this is bullshit."

What better last words? It's almost better than "I'd rather be in Philadelphia."

In the days after her fall, I had to be very good to myself and very good to my mom. And since her death, I've forgiven myself for feeling abandoned by her having dementia and, now, by dying. And I've forgiven myself for my own reaction to all of it. Grief is tricky.

But this doesn't mean you get to say, "I'm just human," and then act like a shit all the time. "I'm just a dick" is not an excuse.

When we are talking about forgiveness and self-forgiveness, what we're really talking about is making a small decision to do better. We're saying, "I'm going to try to be conscious of this. I'm not going to do that anymore. I'm making a promise." When someone accepts an apology, they're accepting that promise, and they are saying that they have empathy about the behavior. This is especially important for recovery, because our addict's monkey mind is so adept at shoving us into the spiral of regret and guilt and shame over and over again if we're not careful.

I had a client, whom I'll call Sam, whose parents are deeply religious. They were born in the old country, and he was born here. Sam is a great guy, and man, is he funny. He's also gay, and his parents are very old school. So Sam, who is a funny, gay, recovering addict has parents who are constantly telling him that his sexuality is just a phase. They say, "You'll change" or "You're only twenty." Or they'll switch it up with, "When are you going to get married?" and "We want grandbabies." At this point, he feels abandoned— worthless in the eyes of his parents. What is Sam to do with that kind of emotional chaos? The answer to this is to either cut his parents out of his life, have his parents in his life while constantly resenting them, or practice forgiveness and see his parents as they are while simultaneously setting up boundaries to protect himself moving forward.

Sam and I talked for a long time about his options. In the end, my biggest question for Sam was this: "Are your parents going to change?" He said he didn't think so. "So," I asked him, "what can you do to make *you* feel okay for the long haul?"

I could see him thinking through the options, and I knew the moment he chose to accept his parents and forgive them, even though they could not accept him. I told him that you don't have to say, "I forgive you for being close-minded people who don't get that I'm a human being." Forgiveness can be changing the way you react to others—the way that you relate to them. It doesn't mean that Sam has to continually subject himself to his parents' disapproval. Sam will need to set really healthy boundaries to shield himself from their disapproval in order to live a life he's comfortable with.

Giving and asking for forgiveness can be hard when it involves family members—"blood is thicker" and all of that. There's this extra expectation that you should just always be okay with everything. But it takes a little bit of forgiveness every day.

With my dad, because I have forgiven him, I accept the past for what it is; and to me, that acceptance and that forgiveness don't mean that what he did was okay. It means that *I* can be okay. I am able to talk about my past, and in doing so, remember some of the hilarious stuff we used to do and acknowledge that he was funny and even kind—the good memories. He also abused me, and there's no changing that. That is what happened. Full stop. Even so, these two realities can coexist through forgiveness.

Asking for (or giving) forgiveness is often linked with making up for the mistake or the damage that was done—in other words, making amends. Clean up your side of the street as best as you can—clean up the things that fall to you to clean—and then live a life that shows you've learned from your choices and that you will do your best to not cause harm again.

When you've actively forgiven yourself, there's a physical feeling—an almost spiritual weightlessness that makes you feel a sense of lightness of being. But self-forgiveness takes a while to get to, and until you do, you just have to bear the weight, even when it feels unbearable sometimes. Grace can help you do that, if you let it.

How do we really gain meaningful forgiveness? By making it tangible, by doing better. Doing better is a lifestyle change based on living a life of integrity and trustworthiness. By living a changed life, we show those we have caused pain that we have changed because we value them. We also show ourselves that we have worth.

The thing with addiction is that when the substance use disorder is active, we do a lot of things that cause others and ourselves pain. More often than not, our own emotional or physical pain is the driving force behind using a substance to dull or cover personal hurt. And then the physiological part of the addiction kicks in and we can't stop. We tell ourselves that we are weak, or that we deserve whatever we get, or a myriad of other horrible things as we pursue our addiction (remember regret, guilt, and shame?). We talk ourselves so far into the ground that it seems true that we're a piece of shit. We do things that underscore that we're shitty, and of course, we do more shitty things to make sure we score—all of which will need to be forgiven, by ourselves or others. And that's scary. It's not an all-at-once proposition; it's a process that you break down into small pieces.

One of the biggest things we have to look at when we look at forgiveness is the tangible outcome. You can't just think it; you have to act. This is deeply connected to our self-esteem and our esteem toward others. When we live a lifestyle of doing better, we do so by doing estimable acts. Estimable acts are those in which you, in small and large ways, show your respect for and recognize the human dignity in others.

Living a changed life starts with your inner dialogue. Begin listening to how you're talking to yourself and how you're talking about the world around you. What are your five most repetitive, cycling negative thoughts throughout the day? Write them down and bring them to your sponsor or counselor to discuss. Find out if they're true. Find out what you can do to shift them a little bit. How are you talking to other people? How is your behavior? Are you reacting or are you responding? Is it the same behavior minus your drug of choice? Are you beginning to change?

If you have trouble changing by thinking about it first, then reverse the process. Start acting like the changed person you want to be, even if you're not feeling it. You know the old adage, "Fake it until you make it"? Try it out. Start doing things that make you proud. It can be as simple as giving someone a mindful smile or a sincere acknowledgment. Or it can be more complex, like regularly and consistently volunteering someplace where you can make a meaningful impact on someone else's life.

Estimable acts create self-esteem and help you understand what it means to "do better."

Forgiveness and living a life with a motto of "do better" is not a been-there-done-that-got-the-T-shirt kind of thing; it's a whole-life thing. Forgiveness—both asking for it and giving it—is a priceless gift. It frees us from the past and helps us create a healthy future. It's a commitment to yourself—a promise you make. It is something you choose every day, and it is something that will make every day worthwhile.

KEEP YOUR PROMISE

Figure out your estimable-acts strategy. Start simple, with something meaningful to you. Slowly grow your list of estimable acts until they fully reflect how you want to do better in your life. Each time you act, think of it as a renewal of your commitment to change and to act with intention.

This is an investment in yourself. In simple terms, you have tremendous inherent value. Every time you act, you're buying stock in yourself.

IT WORKS IF YOU WORK IT

Write a list of things for which you'd like forgiveness from yourself. After you are done, go down that list, and for each item, say out loud, "I forgive myself for . . ." Now write about how it felt to extend forgiveness to yourself.

The Monster Under the Bed

On fear and grace

You had the power all along, my dear.
—Glinda the Good Witch

Early recovery can be scary. But it's not earthquake scary; it's more like that quiet-whisper-in-your-ear scary. And at some point, that whisper is no longer just about using but about being. *Who am I without my sidekick? Am I somebody when I'm not high? What if I don't know who I am? What if I can't separate me from my disorder? What if nobody cares? Oh god, what if I can't do it?*

It's a fear that lightly touches everything as it steals through your thinking and takes up residence in the day-to-day when you go home after treatment. It's the stack of bills on the table that you ignored and the physical wreckage that you created in your environment—the mess, the clothes that are piled up. All reminders of how unmanageable your life had become.

This can be motivating or it can freeze you in your tracks.

Like a tennis volley, the thinking associated with active addiction and the thinking associated with recovery tosses you back and forth. You're bargaining all the time with who you were then and who you are now.

I remember the fear when I first got out of rehab in 1992 and Shane was five. Wow! I was afraid of everything. I was afraid of sex with my husband. I was afraid of being a mom. I was afraid of people. I was hypervigilant all the time, checking in with myself with a running litany: *Am I okay? What should I do next?* All the while being afraid that I didn't know what I was supposed to be doing. I had the tools. I'd been in rehab for nine months, and now it was go time. It was time for the practical application of everything I'd learned. But I remember having a headache and even being afraid of Advil. I was afraid to put a pill in my mouth—afraid that the action in and of itself would trigger something that would make me not be okay anymore. The first time I went to get blood drawn after rehab, I was mortified by the simple act of turning my arm over for the nurse.

In early recovery, you may wake up in a quiet panic, thinking, *Crap. Crap. What should I do?*

The answer is usually something as simple as "get up."

The shift away from that fear happens by way of begetting. One positive action begets another, begets another, begets another. You let the basic things lessen the fear: routine, familiarity, comfort.

Make it super simple; reduce everything down to the next indicated thing, which is something I love because it's something so foreign. When the alarm goes off, the next indicated thing is to start the day. Okay, what does "start the day" mean? You talk yourself through the things that are routine: *I have to pee.* So that's the next thing you should do. Then, *Okay, I've peed, what's next? Oh! I should probably wash my hands. That's a good thing to do.* You walk past the unmade bed when you leave the bathroom, and the next indicated thing to do would be to tidy up the bed. This is where mindfulness comes back around to be your best damn friend in the world.

You begin to take care of the things that you used to neglect or ignore or pretend weren't happening. You develop a routine of thought—like letting the dogs out so they don't pee all over the house like they did when you were using. It's all about doing the next indicated right thing that was begat from the previous right thing. You cultivate this routine of thought, and by doing so, you start to reset your life's clock.

It's the little things that will help you stick to this. Set aside time to deal with the wreckage—the pile of bills that we all talk about and then ignore. Set aside time for a reasonable list of goals: *Today, I'm going to begin to tackle this, and I'm not going to let myself get all into the chaos of starting one thing and moving to another, and then ending up with a bigger mess than I had to begin with. I'm just gonna make progress on this one thing.*

I remember when I first got sober. I'd be at a 12-step meeting at nine in the morning and then at the next meeting in the same building at ten thirty. Then there was one at noon. Then there was one at three. That took me to four o'clock, where it was like, "Okay, by four o'clock, I think I can do the rest of this day."

It wasn't that I was dying to go out and get high or get drunk right at four; it was that I wasn't quite sure how to fill the time. I needed to observe and interact with other people who had actually done it. That's where the fellowship of a recovery program is incredibly useful. In early recovery, it's a lot of monkey see, monkey do. Just be sure you're watching the right monkey.

At four, I'd stand on the sidewalk and chat with my fellow recovering addicts. Invariably, I'd get in my car, turn it on, and the clock would say 4:20. I'd laugh to myself. *How fucking ironic is this? I'm on my way home from spending an entire day at AA meetings, and the clock says 4:20?* Then, all of a sudden, everything was manageable from there on out. *It's 4:20. Okay. I'm gonna go home and start dinner. I'm gonna get settled in and feed the dogs, and then do the dishes, and then maybe read. I can do this on my own now. If I can make it to 4:20, I'm home free.*

All of this was because of my fear of just being. What's interesting about fear is that it can be subtle or it can be blatant. It can show up as anger or sadness or over-the-the-top cheerfulness. It tries to disguise itself in cockiness or self-confidence, or it can slip on the mask of painful shyness. We sometimes express our fear in these other ways and don't even understand that, really, we're not angry, we're scared.

Fear makes us feel tremendously vulnerable because fear is the result of feeling like there is something dangerous nearby—something that might cause pain. For an addict, the dangerous thing is found in the addictive behaviors, falling into old ways of thinking, going back to using. It's feeling that you're dangerous to yourself, that you might cause yourself harm.

What do we do with that? How does a person learn to manage a fear of themselves? The answer is that you must have a shift in perception. I think it's a little different for everyone, but I like to think of it as grace. But grace is so hard to pin down that I'm going to run through different ways to see grace and to identify it, so you can see it for yourself.

Grace is defined many ways. Grace is poise, elegance, forgiveness, or a blessing. Grace can be defined as honoring, a sense of what is right and proper, as decency, as thoughtfulness toward others, as goodwill and favor. An example of grace is letting go of a past wrong done to you. Another example of grace is the way a beautiful, stylish woman easily walks across the room.[1]

To me, grace is a deep spiritual sense that everything is going to be okay but with joy—a quiet joy. Grace and the perceptive distance it gives allows us to manage our fear. It allows us to see a moment from a place of nonjudgment and with clarity. It allows us to see clearly the moment and ourselves within it. You can have it if you choose to be open to it. You can access it. You can even begin to practice it.

Grace is a certain openness. It's also about being able to take a hit in life and, when everyone would expect you to be angry and get up swinging, still maintain a sense of serenity. It allows you to hold steady to that serenity (versus before, when you were like a wobbly and fragile bird). It's about being able to hold the self in a stable position, even in the face of fear.

That said, grace isn't always pretty. Grace is the ability to continue even when you feel like life has beaten you black and blue. By the time you get back on your feet, you're a sweaty mess, barely able to drag yourself on. Within that space, it's grace that is the ability and resilience and energy that drives you to move forward.

It manifests in little ways, like when I say yes to an invitation I was thinking of declining because saying yes would mean I'd have to wake up at the butt crack of dawn. Part of me thinks, *Crap, I've got to set my alarm for six thirty in the morning*, but then grace allows me to do it.

Grace can be the feel of your dog's fuzzy head resting under your palm as you wind down from your day. It can be sharing a joke with your child or watching them accomplish something they care about. It can be found in unexpectedly tearing up during a breathtaking piece of music.

Grace is a steady light. If you're on a boat that's moving on the waves, grace is the steady beacon on the shore that never wavers, no matter how dark the night gets. When the water is calm, finding grace is easy. But sometimes, a storm brews up, and it's a struggle to stay on course, let alone look for the light. I think sometimes, when you can't feel grace, you're turned the wrong way. It's there—you've simply lost sight of it. Grace is always there, and it's always within reach. We just have to remember to turn toward it, even when we can't see it.

Grace has saved me more than once. It has been there every time I've overdosed. It has been there for every rock bottom. It has filled me with compassion when I thought I'd run dry. It has filled me with purpose when I thought I had none.

Grace is fear's balance. If fear is the dark unknown, then grace is the light that you move toward.

I had a moment one time when I was driving through the Sonoran Desert in Arizona. I was heading from California to New Mexico to stay with some friends. It was just at dusk, and the silhouettes of the saguaro cactuses seemed like hands rising up from land to sky. I had dogs in the back, in that loose-limbed sleep of utter relaxation that dogs do, and I had put the windows down, the air just cool enough to finally turn off the AC. I put my hand out the window, sailing it through the air, and watched the stars slowly emerge until the night sky was full of them, and the sweep of the Milky Way arched across.

I felt both endless and finite. I felt raw and new in the moment, full of a sense of connection to the world around me and a sense of all-being. This was the holy, the spiritual—my dogs, the universe, and me, together and expansive. I pulled over without any thought; I wanted to just look and be, just for a while. I got out of the front seat and crawled into the back, gently gathered the dogs until I could feel the warmth of their bodies, their breathing and heartbeats, and just looked at the sky, the stars, the saguaros reaching up.

I felt the moment down into my toes and up into my head until it was all of me and all of me was everything that was around me. It was a beautiful moment, and there was grace in it. But the grace wasn't the moment itself; it was that I was able to see and feel the moment, recognize the breadth of it. It was grace that allowed me to really see the sky, the desert, and myself.

If I had been using, I would have flown by it all. None of this would have pinged my radar. Not one bit. When I think about that, I think, *How awful*, and I wonder how many such moments I missed over the years while I was high. I'm determined not to lose what grace has let me see. I'm afraid to not see.

We think of fear as a weakness, which it can be if we let it. But fear should be used as a tool, an early warning system that reminds us to be careful. When you are in early recovery and feel like every-thing is dangerous, that's when you're most vulnerable. Your fear is saying, "You should be careful; you should be mindful."

If we let fear overwhelm us, it freezes us in place or it sends us packing. As you begin recovery, be aware that there are certain fears that are common for all of us. The idea here is to not cut and run and start using again if you feel them. Here's the short list of things you might fear in recovery:[2]

- Fear that life will not be enjoyable again (particularly prominent during early sobriety)

- Fear that staying sober will require too much effort
- Fear of journeying into unknown territory
- Fear of facing life challenges without a chemical crutch
- Fear of failure or, alternately, success
- Fear of rejection
- Fear of death
- Fear of losing your identity
- Fear of facing financial and career concerns

Flip that shit! Own your recovery.

Fortunately, there are ways to manage your fears. Some of the techniques I've used are pretty straightforward—stuff like identifying exactly what I was afraid of. One way I figured that out was to make a list. It wasn't quick going, though; I really had to be thoughtful about it and do some inner investigating since fear can be disguised as other strong emotions. Examine your anger, sadness, overconfidence, shyness, and other overwhelming feelings to see if they might actually be fear.

Fear loses strength when it's brought out into the open, so I reached out for help when I was feeling overwhelmed. I talked to my sponsor and my therapist and my people—the more the merrier! My fear lost its stranglehold the more I knew I wasn't alone and that others had experienced it too. I sought out grace and held on to it when I found it.

I also started to look at fear as a place of teaching. I asked myself what my fear was trying to tell me. The key here, I found out, is to not be reactive; just listen and try to find out what is driving that fear. See if there is a lesson to be learned.

I practiced being mindful and did a little meditation too. Being mindful helped me stay calm, focused, and in touch with the now. Fear is about preparing us for danger by projecting us into what might happen. Staying in the now helped me manage this anxiety.

There are lots of different ways to approach fear as you travel through your recovery, especially since your needs and your fears will change over time. Like everything else in life, there are layers to our fears. In much the same way, there are layers to grace and where we find it, how we identify with it, and how it changes our perceptions and our ability to continue on. Just remember that fear, though unbearable at times, is actually there to protect you. Observe it; learn from it. Try to see it in a new, more graceful light.

When I was working on this chapter and thinking about fear, I kept going back to when I was a little girl—really little—and how I would have horrific night terrors. I remember waking up crouched between the toilet and the shower stall in my mom's house. I had this deep, anxious fear in my dream because I was supposed to gather 147 watermelons but only had 146. I feared something bad was going to happen to me because I hadn't gathered enough watermelons. I don't know what it was that I was so afraid of—I mean, come on, watermelons? But the fear was overwhelming. Paralyzing. Truly terrifying.

Looking back on those terrors, I realize that, even at seven or eight years old, I was scared of failure. Of not being good enough. Crouched down on the bathroom floor in my little nightie covered in bows and ribbons, shaking. Sometimes I'm still that little frightened child—we all are.

Fear for addicts is all too real. We've met the monsters under our bed. But don't freeze. Don't you freeze. Don't run. Take a moment. Be mindful. What is your fear trying to say to you?

Work the process. Trust your support network. Be aware. Be mindful.

Here's the truth: when you're freaking out about monsters or watermelons, you've got to take a leap that's inspired by grace. The final thing that your fear can teach you is to remember that there is always hope on the other side.

FINDING GRACE

Knowing when grace is in action can be hard. Harder still is to flip the switch that lets you see it. One of the things that really helps is to think about what you're grateful or thankful for. Make a list. Find and acknowledge one beautiful thing that's happened in every day. These things don't have to be monumental; they can be full of the mundane day-to-day stuff. For instance, I'm really grateful for coffee. (Everyone say "Amen!" to that one.) You get what I'm saying.

Actively looking for these kinds of things will open you up to the grace that surrounds you. There's beauty in the ordinary.

IT WORKS IF YOU WORK IT

Write about a situation in your life that brought you fear. How did you survive? That survival is where the grace was. Now write about what is currently bringing you fear. Based on past survival, can you see where the grace in this situation might be?

Fifty Years of Denial

On abuse and trauma

*I wonder how much of what weighs me down
isn't mine to carry.*

—**Anonymous**

This chapter will be different than the other chapters in that I will attempt to avoid evoking something that might take you to a not-so-great place, while continuing to be as straightforward as I can. If you've experienced childhood abuse, also called childhood trauma or maltreatment, or if you've experienced abuse or trauma as an adult, I strongly encourage you to talk to someone you trust before reading this and then talk to them again immediately after you have finished reading this. Why? Because if you've experienced maltreatment or violence, sometimes reading about it can trigger associations with your own experiences. Emotional safety is important, and I want to make sure you take care of you.

Here's the hardcore truth: you can smash the pipe, put the plug in the jug, break the tip off the needle, but if you don't address the deeper issues, you're not going to be able to get whole or become a healthy part of the world around you. Trauma, maltreatment, or abuse, whatever you choose to call it, is a huge, deeper issue that comes up a lot when we look at addiction. Not talking about trauma and its relationship to substance use would be like avoiding the larger-than-normal elephant in the room. Childhood trauma and its aftermath is something that needs to be spoken of and brought out into the open. This is also true of adult trauma, which is often not spoken of or reported. If you've experienced childhood abuse, you've probably kept it or have been keeping it secret for a long time, which can do you damage in the form of, well, gee, stuff like addiction. If you're a perpetrator and you actually know that you are one, then you've probably gone out of your way try to hide the elephant. To that I say stop and no.

What I've learned over time is that not addressing the trauma you've been exposed to and just addressing the addiction (or whatever other toxic behavior we're trying to overcome) keeps you from truly getting better. Honestly, I think that I stayed sober for those ten years before I relapsed by force of will alone, because I certainly hadn't addressed my own childhood trauma in any effective way. And I know that I relapsed because I was still living with the pain it caused me.

In my case, I had a childhood rife with traumas that rocked my worldview. One was neglect by my parents, and the other was being raped by a stranger as a teenager. Both caused profound pain—pain that I sought to numb. For here and now, I'm going to be speaking primarily about my experience with neglect.

Neglect can wear many masks. I had a lot of clothes and a house-keeper and food. I had an attentive and amazing mom when she wasn't drunk or hung over or getting abused. I also had a tortured father who was kind when he was around, but that didn't happen often. Most of the time, he was unaware that his kids, my brother and I, were basically free-range kids when we stayed with him.

I, like many who are neglected as children, never considered myself to be abused or, for that matter, neglected. It's even hard for me to say it now. I didn't recognize it; it was just my life. It's sometimes hard to talk about—I mean, look at my childhood: I was privileged. It's still awkward to manage the duality of that; sometimes I call it "fancy neglect" in my head, so I can have a way to express the two sides of my childhood for myself.

Once, I was at a screening of *American Graffiti* at the Director's Guild of America. There was a Q&A with George Lucas and Candy Clark, and all the people who were in the movie were there. Afterward, during the mingling, the producer of the film, Gary Kurtz, whom I hadn't seen in decades, came up to me and said, "Do you remember when you got off the plane in San Francisco, and you were twelve and you were alone?" I gave him a blank look, maybe mixed with a con-fused face. I had no idea what he was talking about.

So he launched into this story I'd never heard before: "Yeah, you arrived in San Francisco. We came to pick you up at the airport, and you got off the plane with a little suitcase at twelve years old, all by yourself. And we said, 'Wait, where's your legal guardian?' And you said, 'I don't know. My mom just put me on a plane.'"

From there, he went on to tell me about how they almost had to recast me because I couldn't live alone as a minor. So Gary ended up becoming my legal guardian for the filming, and I lived with his family and him while the movie was being made.

As he told me the story, I felt this uncomfortable feeling slide through me. It made me want to shift around on my feet and roll my shoulders to shake off the discomfort. I had no idea what Gary was talking about.

Looking back at that, I get that my lack of memory of that flight, the ensuing drama, and the unsettled feeling in being asked to recall it was a response to something that I had found traumatizing as a young person. My inability to remember the situation is a good indicator of how unsafe I must have felt getting on that plane and going alone into the world at the age of twelve. When I think about it now, I try to imagine what my younger self felt. What did it feel like to have to rely on strangers to step in to take care of me because my parents didn't or wouldn't do it? How did my twelve-year-old self internalize that? Did I feel abandoned? Did I question my value to my parents? Did I feel ashamed? Whatever I felt at the time, the combo was enough for me to block that memory out entirely. I still have literally no memory of that dramatic moment from my childhood.

It took years and some help from someone else for me to identify that the high level of instability and lack of consistent parental presence in my childhood was a chronic trauma that I had normalized and created behaviors to compensate for.

There were different times in my life that I recognized that my childhood was less than ideal in terms of the relationship I had with my parents, but I didn't deal with it. Mostly, I made excuses for it and shoved the emotional pain down deep to avoid it. Or I took drugs because then I wouldn't feel any pain at all in any way. I also think the excitement of my life, the outer representation of all that was glittery, was a great distractor as well. I was a TV star, and I had money—which could buy me drugs.

All of that was easier to focus on than the internal pain. All the way up until I wrote *High on Arrival*, when I truly saw my life for the first time. It was a wake-up call. Until then, I didn't even know I was self-medicating the pain from being a child of neglect. I thought that what I felt like was just life. That's what childhood trauma does to you: it normalizes pain, and you end up finding mechanisms to numb the consistent feeling of hurt—hurt that is felt both in your heart and in your body.

After *High on Arrival* came out, and everyone and their uncle was commenting and theorizing on how what had happened could have happened with my dad, and my reaction to it was scrutinized by the press, I would lie in my bed at night, thinking, *What have I done?* It was a pretty classic response: the victim of the trauma taking responsibility for all of it.

It made me realize there was more work to be done and that just puking out my story wasn't going to heal me. It was the first step, but it wasn't going to do the job. If I was going to be well, happy, sober, and useful to the community at large, I had to do some deep work. And that was scary because I thought just the retelling of it would be enough. But it wasn't.

The deep work was hard and complex. The complex part doesn't go away either, especially if it's about your parents. To this day, I still don't know how to fully talk about my dad. It's tangled and compli-cated, and my feelings for him and the things that happened range across a spectrum of emotions. One week I might be okay with talking about it, and the next, not so much. This shit is complicated. It's work—god, is it work sometimes—to find my center and ground myself in what I know is healthy. I know that all of my childhood and adult traumas live within me. Sometimes they're light, and sometimes they feel as heavy as a herd of elephants. And that's what it is, light and heavy. Just that.

Over the course of my time working with clients as well as with my own experiences, I've learned a lot about childhood trauma. A lot of it's pretty disturbing. The statistics give us some hard facts, such as childhood maltreatment happens at the rate of nine out of every one thousand children in the United States. That's over 700,000 children! And just in one year.[1] I've also learned that abuse can take many forms. Here are some truly disturbing percentages of children who experienced maltreatment from a one-year sample: 79.5 percent of children abused were neglected; 18 percent were physically abused; 9 percent were sexually abused; 8.7 percent were psychologically abused; 10 percent were abused in some other way. Now, if you do the math, you will notice that the percentages here add up to more than 100 percent. This is because some children were victims of multiple types of abuse.[2]

Here's another depressing fact: up to 59 percent of young people with childhood trauma end up developing substance abuse problems, and the majority of those who do are female.[3] So I was a statistical probability (good to know).

The bottom line is that when there is an underlying trauma that accompanies a substance use disorder, there is always additional work to be done. It goes like this: first we aim for stabilization and creating a safe environment, and then we start looking at the underlying issues.

Trauma, much like addiction, messes with the brain on a physiological level. It rewires shit up there and then reinforces it with a repeat-and-rinse cycle that is truly epic. Close your eyes and picture a country road with grass, trees, and wagon wheel tracks in the grass. For hundreds of years, wagon wheels went down the same track, and there are deep ruts in that beautiful country road. Can you can see it?

Those are the neural pathways that trauma has created in the brain. A traumatized person's brain is so tuned to those tracks that, when it gets triggered or stimulated, it goes straight to the most embedded path—those rutted wagon wheel tracks. But there are billions of other connections our brain can make because we have something called psychoneuroplasticity, which is to say that our brains can reroute. But to do this, there needs to be a disruption.

It's like a vinyl record that has a skip in it: we need to move the needle off that track. Trauma manifests differently for different people, so treatment will be different for different people. There are a variety of methods, and the method should be customized to match the needs of the individual. This is something that you and your counselor should discuss at great length. Whatever method is used, the main idea is to disrupt the trauma path in the brain and help it jump to another connection—to knock it off the groove in the record, allowing you to have other responses.

When we experience trauma, our brains go into a different kind of gear—a survival mode that is built to make sure we make it out of a harmful situation alive. It also catalogues all of the things that surround the trauma so that it can sound the alarm if it feels like you're in a similar situation. I had a client who had been assaulted while the phone was ringing in the background, so one of her major triggers was the ringing of a phone. The sound was something that her brain alarmed to, and when the phone rang, she would go straight into high survival mode. Given how often a phone rings in our lives, it isn't a surprise that she developed unhealthy coping mechanisms to get through a day.

Part of coping with trauma is a deep internalization of it. We may act it out in some way, shape, or form that is seeable by others, but it's like an iceberg: what you see above the surface is nothing compared to the beast floating underneath the surface.

Deep trauma hollows you. It feels like some vital aspect of yourself, like marrow, has been pulled out, and you know you are fragile, broken, wounded. You live waiting for the blow—it doesn't matter if it's emotional or physical—that will take you down. Maybe what we feel being pulled out is the who-we-would-have-been self. It's missing but still felt, like a phantom limb.

Because childhood trauma—indeed any trauma—creates such havoc, we carry it with us for the rest of our lives. There is that before-trauma you and then there comes the after-trauma you. It's marked on your life's map, a demarcation that shows a forced and unchosen change in your route.

I once heard abuse being compared to murder because the person who that child or adult could have been has been irrevocably lost due to someone else's unjustifiable action. I don't know how I feel about that comparison overall, but what I do know is that abuse changes how a person sees and acts in the world; and it is something that changes survivors in a way that stays changed. This shows up in both good and bad ways. Usually, the bad comes first. Trauma and abuse often disrupt us enough that we lose some or all of our self-regulating skills. How could it not? It takes work and time to find the path to good.

So, how do we manage the aftermath of something as big as all of that?

First things first, because we're also talking about substance use here, you need to get stabilized and safe before you start tackling this stuff. This is because there is a strong chance that your addiction is triggered by the things that bring up the traumatic event for you.

Second, recognize that trauma takes up residence not only in your mind but also in your body. Think about it like this: we're housed in sinew and bone, muscle and skin. Our bodies hold us to the here and now; they are where we live. Our lives are mapped in our bodies, each scar a story. Each scar related to some sort of pain. Some of our stories, we carry where they can be seen; some of our stories are held deeper. And for all of it, your body keeps score. It comes out in headaches; pain in your joints; stomach issues; weight issues; feelings of exhaustion, anxiety, and depression. I had somatic experiences. I had chronic pain. I had quick-trigger anger. I had deep defensiveness. I had huge judgment, which is something we all, as humans, still have bits and pieces of. Trauma is an interior wound that bleeds out into everything else yet is often not recognized as the source of all of the things that are happening to you physically and emotionally.

With abuse, the wound is on the inside, and it's raw and open. We create a facade that allows us to feel like our vulnerability is being protected. This is a defense mechanism much like how our brains create overactive alarm systems. This facade is our trauma self, the part of ourselves that comes to the fore when we feel like we are in an emotionally unsafe place. And feeling unsafe can come from anything. Maybe it's that something doesn't go as expected or someone dies or we get into a fight with a friend. Whatever it might be— *boom!*—our trauma self emerges. That's when relapse can occur. But know this: even if you don't pick up a drink or a drug, you might still act out on old behaviors; you may still act to protect the wound that's still bleeding.

The third thing to do is to tell someone. A counselor or therapist is recommended, but you can start with just sharing with a trusted friend. You don't have to go deep into it right away; just start by sharing that you had a rough childhood or traumatic experience that you still carry with you. If you don't want to share it with someone else, then acknowledge it for yourself, *with* yourself.

The fourth thing is to let go of any shame and feelings of responsibility you might have. Abuse and trauma are never, ever the fault of the person who was abused or traumatized. *Ever.*

The power dynamic between the abuser and the survivor is not equal. In all cases, the abuser holds the power and the survivor is disempowered or never had any power to begin with. If it's the power dynamic between a child and a caregiver, then the dynamic set within that relational space will favor the caregiver, no matter the age of the child. In other words, even a fully grown person will still see their parents as having more power, and the parents will still act as if their child has less. This is how abuse happens, even after children become adults. In every case, when you've been stripped of choice or never had a choice, and have no power in a situation, you're not responsible for what happens. The shame of it is not yours, nor is the blame. It belongs with the person who, while in a position of greater power, chose to abuse that power and harm the person who was less powerful.

Finally, let yourself feel the pain for what it is. Part of the reason the wound is still open is because you learned to hide it away instead of heal it. Case in point, historically, when I was sharing my trauma with a therapist back in the day, I was very blasé about it. I wasn't at all connected to it. It was like two separate versions of me, and the one talking would say very matter-of-factly this happened and that happened and this happened and that happened, but it was like I was talking about somebody else. I lived with my wound bleeding all over the place while I told my story over and over again, and never actually did anything about it. It was just the telling of it. It became rote.

I was so dissociated from the pain of it. I could talk about it, but I couldn't process it. It wasn't until after *High on Arrival* when it became so clear to me that there was some work to do—that I was actually able to connect to it instead of being dispassionately narrative about it.

I see this a lot with clients. They can narrate their trauma to me without having a connection to it; it's purely a self-preservation thing. As addicts, drugs and alcohol help facilitate that distance. These substances help build and maintain a wall and a brain that can narrate without feeling.

They say we rarely change unless our backs are up against the wall and the pain becomes so great that we can't go on as we are. And yet we feel like if we do anything about our pain, we're going to die. It's that visceral.

In the end, there was a moment when I fully realized that my own experience with trauma and abuse, even after so much time had passed, was still a presence living in my life. I mean, Jesus, I'd be driving along on an average day, and all of a sudden, the trauma loop would get caught up in my head. It would be like a video of a traumatic event in my life that I was watching. It would feel as if it was happening again. I would cringe from fear, from shame, from the pain of it. This is just me driving down the street, cringing in my car, feeling almost paralyzed from all of it. I would try to figure out what had triggered it. Was it a particular road sign? The name of a street? A song on the radio? Or had my wandering thoughts just taken me to one of the well-worn pathways in my brain?

But then I had a moment, *that* moment, a leap-of-faith moment: I realized that if I didn't do some work, I would go back to what I knew, which was shooting coke. My inner self had a conversation that went kind of like, *Okay, look. Either you're going to continue to do things as you've been doing them to mask your pain, which means that you're going to relapse, or you're going to finally actually do something about this interior wound you've got bleeding all over the place. What are you going to do?* It was the get-off-the-pot-or-do-your-business kind of speech.

That was my moment. I had finally told the full story in *High on Arrival*, and now, finally, I was going to do something about the trauma I had been living with my whole life. I had allowed myself to feel the pain, to see and accept it with grace. Now, I knew, I had to get on top of that shit.

I went to counseling and, after discussing it with my therapist, I did eye movement desensitization and reprocessing (EMDR) therapy, which is a therapy that is used to reduce the long-term effects of trauma by interrupting the automatic jump the brain makes to the rutted wagon path.[4] It was a treatment that worked for me. Other kinds of very effective treatments are also out there, so use whatever you and your recovery team decide works best for you. My treatment helped me break not just my own cycle of thinking but also a cycle of abuse—one that I had inherited from my mom and my dad, both of whom had their own traumas bleeding all over the place.

As mentioned, other things are super effective. One of those things is group work (again, this is something to go over with your therapist or counselor). Groups can be a safe place to talk about how you've been processing your trauma. They allow you to see other people who are living with it too—people who you can listen to and learn from. Sometimes it's enough just to hear someone else articulate a feeling or way of thinking that you had never spoken out loud for yourself before. Things like that can be pretty profound. Finding the words to express not just the experience but the feelings connected to your experience is empowering. Even more so is the realization that you don't have to keep the secret anymore. Something I've noticed when I do groups with my clients is how much benefit everyone in the group gets—the amount of healing they experience just by virtue of witnessing someone else's healing. It's sometimes mind blowing, watching the breakthroughs that happen.

There's a theme going on here, that theme being getting help through therapy. All of the available therapy is there to help you gain healthy behaviors that will help reduce and manage the impact of a trauma, whether it be from chronic childhood maltreatment or from a single trauma event. Notice I said help you reduce and manage the impact; there isn't a cure-all, fix-it, magic thing that makes it all go away. I'm not going to candy-coat it. Working through trauma and abuse can be harrowing and emotionally exhausting. You're going to want to stop. *Don't*. Midway through, you're going to think you've learned enough and can go it alone. *You haven't.* The thing is, with trauma, until you do all of the work, you don't really see that the trauma has stopped. You have to find a way to see the whole iceberg without feeling the panic and fear, without being overwhelmed with the memories and pain of it all. Then you can see that it had a beginning, a middle, and most important, an end. Don't get me wrong—there will be good days and bad days. But you will be able to work your way through them in a healthy way. You will have the power to do so.

If you have experienced and are still experiencing the pain caused by abuse or trauma at any age, and you have that hollowed-out feeling—that emptiness that we keep on trying to fill up—I would like you to change how you think about that hollowness. Flip the meaning on it and think about it in a different way. What if that hollowness is not about something that needs to be replaced? Think of a bird, with its hollow bones, and its surprising strengths and amazing abilities. The amazing endurance it has to fly great distances; the resilience it has that allows it to fall from a nest and still get back up. Think about how birds dive and rise back up—how they glide on secret airways. Birds have hollow bones so that they can fly.

We can't put back what was taken. We will never be the before-the-trauma person that we would have been. What's done is past, and that is unchangeable. What we can do is choose how we move forward. I say we should fly.

CONNECTING ALL THE PIECES

One of the biggest things that happens with abuse or trauma is dissociation. We disconnect the emotions that we felt at the time of the trauma from the memory of the trauma. Unfortunately, it's hard to compartmentalize that coping mechanism, so we start to dissociate ourselves from any strong feelings and, often, our lives in general. One of the simplest things you can start to do is to check in with yourself throughout the day and ask yourself, *How am I feeling?*

The key here is to not be half-assed about it. Take a moment and really think about your feelings. If you have to, write down a list of emotions so that you can put a word to what you are feeling. It can be a simple list like *sad, scared, panicked, angry, happy, joyful, calm.*

When we start connecting our emotions to ourselves again, we begin to make ourselves whole.

IT WORKS IF YOU WORK IT

Sometimes it's hard to start talking about your trauma to a counselor or a sponsor. If you are having difficulty opening up about your trauma, try writing down a simple statement. It can be as simple as "I was abused." Once you do, ask your sponsor if you can read what you wrote. This will help you open up the conversation that needs to follow.

Hey, You're Only Human

On making goals, having a bad day,

and what happens next

Fall seven times, stand up eight.
—Japanese proverb

We all have bad days. Hell, we sometimes have bad weeks or months. We all revert back on occasion to a former self that we have fought to overcome. It's a part of being human.

It's the same with being sober. There are good days and there are bad days. There are days when you feel safe and days when you don't. Sometimes you feel like you can stay sober and sometimes you're scared shitless that you can't. I don't mean craving or wanting to get high; alcohol and drug use are just symptoms of a deeper underlying issue. I mean days when old behaviors come to the fore because of issues we are dealing with. It's when the behaviors pop up that you know you're struggling. It can be getting stressed out and deciding to ditch your responsibilities to relieve that stress. It can be lying about how much work you have to do to avoid going out with a friend. Those might be behaviors you did when you were using. If those pop up, know you're on notice—you're on notice because you know that a part of being sober is showing up for your responsibilities and your commitments, even if you'd rather be doing something else. Really working at being sober means that when you do suit up and show up no matter how you feel, you can feel good about the fact you did.

I remember once when the light bulb in my refrigerator was burned out for three years, and I didn't care. It was okay with me. I'd be rooting around in a dark refrigerator when I had the fucking light bulb on the shelf in the pantry. It was a part of a pattern of self-neglect that I learned to recognize. It's not okay with me anymore to root around in the dark. When the light bulb burns out, I replace it. It's little things like that that are indicators to me of my wellness. That's the difference between active addiction and active recovery.

I now know my behaviors in the same way I know the sounds my house makes. I didn't when I moved in, but now it's fifteen years later. These particular sounds of a house built in 1927 were disturbing and scary to me at first. Now I say hello to them; they comfort me. This awareness, this knowledge, allows me to know when something's wrong. I know when a sound doesn't belong.

There are things you can do to keep bad days to a minimum. One of the biggest things that has always helped me was creating structure. Structure is important because, generally, the addict or the alcoholic, when actively in the addiction, doesn't really have a schedule unless they're very functional. Creating a daily routine that has you getting up and doing your recovery-based activities with reliability is really important. One of the worst things an addict can do is to have a bunch of free time on their hands. It leaves them room to swing back into their old way of thinking and being without structure; it can create a rudderless feeling that prohibits mindfulness. You end up feeling out of sync and out of time when you don't have a clear routine, which leaves you feeling as if you're not really present. There is a rhythm to a routine that is almost musical: the forward motion, the syncopation of a task well done followed by a moment of rest, then the beginning again. We all march to the beat of a different drummer. Are you marching to the beat of death metal, with its relentless pulsing; or are you marching to the beat of singer-songwriter music, with its mellow melodies? What's your rhythm? If you're always going at a relentless pace, maybe get into a more relaxed rhythm instead of the thrash rhythm.

Take your self-accountability seriously, because you're only really accountable to yourself. Create reasonable goals, and try to reach them—*reasonable* is key here. I have a lot of clients who are like, "Okay, so first day I get out, here's my list," and there'll be like eighty-five things to do on that list. That's not a list, that's a book! "Eight o'clock in the morning, I'm going to go for a run. Then I'm going to call fifteen people in the program. And then I'm going to go to the noon meeting. Then I'm going to cook a gourmet lunch for my mother. And then I'm going to go to Target and I'm going to finish my—" Whoa, whoa, whoa! Slow down. You're going to burn out after about number three of the eighty-five. Save the other eighty-two for later. Create realistic, actionable goals that won't make you shoot your accountability in the foot. Keep it small, keep it incremental—don't set yourself up for failure. Practice awareness of what you're doing, when you're doing it, why you're doing it, and what the purpose of doing it is.

Sometimes the cure for a bad day, as crazy as is sounds, is to just find something you like doing. I was driving home the other day and noticed that my hands were clenched so hard on the steering wheel that it felt like a death grip. I checked in with myself and realized I was stressed out from having a harder-than-normal day—one that had left me emotionally wrung out and wrapped up in the vulnerability of the people I had counseled that day. I hit a red light and started to self-soothe. I sat there in my car, thinking that I needed to let it go . . . *It's not happening to me, it's happening around me; and I can either choose to internalize someone else's pain and fear or I can let it be theirs.* Then I remembered it was a Monday and *The Voice* was on that night, which gave me something positive to fix my mind on and look forward to.

Sometimes after work, Shane and I have a dog party. I'll look at him and go, "Dog party," and he'll nod and say, "Dog party." We sit on the floor in the dining room, and we just let the dogs run all around us. We talk about them, and we kiss them. It's really just about getting a love fest on—something as simple as that. What makes a bad day better is singular to the individual; you've got to figure it out yourself. But it's certainly not a drink or a shot.

Remember that it's okay to seek your own safety; just be mindful that it's not limiting you to a wider experience. A lot of my interactions are with people and things that I deem safe—my cats and dogs and people that are familiar—and that's okay. It's okay to choose your tribe.

A lot of feeling safe is creating predictability for yourself. One of the best ways to do that is to create routines—we've talked about them. Get yourself some—and don't be shy about it either. Just as I have a practice to begin my days, I have one to end them. It helps to bring a state of balance and positive routine to my life. As I'm on my way home from work, there's a moment when I get off the freeway at my exit when I'm like, "Phew! Fuck, I made it. No more traffic!" I pull up in front of the house, and I think, *My dogs are in there. Shane's in there.* I come in, and I try to be very quiet because I don't want to set off the bark fest. I put my keys down. I put my briefcase down. And I just take a moment and think, *Home is the best place in the world.* When I'm at work, I need to *be* at work; and when I'm at home, I need to *be* at home. I take a moment to recognize this and shift from workspace to home space. Then I'll walk back down the hall toward Shane's room, and the dogs will hear me.

The first thing I'll do is say hi to Shane and then I close his door. Then I let the dogs out in the backyard. Then I go sit in Shane's room, and we visit—we talk about our day. There are back rubs and hugs and kisses on cheeks; there's a "Hi, Mom" and a "Hi, Sweetie," and a "How was your day?" back and forth. Then I'll let the dogs back in for the inevitable bark fest followed closely by the lick fest. It's the best welcome back to where I belong.

Then I always say to Shane, "I'm going to go change out of my monkey suit," because I call my work clothes my monkey suit. Once I'm in my home clothes, I'll go out and set up the grind-and-brew for the next morning. I'll flip through the mail. I'll do the dishes that are in the sink. It's a nice time to just settle back in and do my thing. Boring? Maybe. Just what I need? Pretty damn close.

When you've had a bad day—when your shit's been knocked off the table and nothing seemed to go right for you—it's also good to know that there are tons of ways to release endorphins through physical activity. You can release endorphins and alleviate your mood with movement. If you raise your arms up over your head and hold that pose for a while, it will release endorphins. Try it! Stand up and raise your hands up over your head. Hold that for two minutes. If you're like me, you probably started to rock and sway while you stood there. Shake around and dance a little if it strikes you.

After you've finished, sit for a minute and feel how you are. Did it elevate your mood just a tad? If it didn't work, try doing it naked while jumping up and down. If you do that, at the bare minimum, you'll get to laugh at yourself, which can be the best mood lifter and stress ass-kicker ever. Nothing like being willfully ridiculous to elevate the mood.

Which brings me to finding humor in things—even if it's dark humor. Laughter is just outright healing. It's easier to get to than you think because, if we look closely, most things have a certain level of absurdity to them. I dance with my dogs when I'm feeling restless or scatterbrained. I'll turn up the music and shake around the couch to an audience of confused but supportive pugs and chihuahuas. (I know they believe in me even if no one's gonna be calling me for *So You Think You Can Dance* anytime soon.) You can dance like nobody's watching. (Well, you can at least dance like nobody's watching but a bunch of deeply, deeply confused canines.) It never fails to lift me up into a space filled with humor—a space that even feels a little bit like grace.

It helps that humor and laughter are just other faces of hope.

Hope is where we started, so hope is where we'll end.

I'm going to close where I started the book by saying that I am—*we* are—more than our substance use disorder. We're regular people with all of the regular people things to deal with. We just sometimes have a little something more to add to our regular stuff.

During the course of this book, we've covered lots of things—from mindfulness to fear, from trust to shame. I've used lots of metaphors to try to help explain things, and I've used my own life to show examples. I've spoken about hope, grace, and faith; and I don't think I've done them justice in the measure of what those three things are capable of doing for us—but I sure did try.

I've talked about addiction as a sidekick and passenger, and recovery as a road. I've used watercolors and sweatshirts with kittens on them and leaping into the unknown and steady lights on the shore to explain concepts that can be nebulous until you've experienced them for yourself.

I've also given things to think about and some examples of what has worked for me. It is my most sincere hope that, in some small way, what you've read here has helped you on your journey to recovery.

The stone-cold truth is that recovery is *hard*. It takes an enormous amount of dedication to get there and stay there. Finding your motivation is huge. The motivation itself can be as simple or as complex as you need it to be. Hell, one of my greatest motivators that helped with my recovery was that tomato jam at the staff table at Alina Lodge.

You will never work so hard at something in your entire life as you strive for recovery every day. The most important thing is to never give up, even if you stumble. Brush that shit off and get back on the horse. In *Full Catastrophe Living*, Jon Kabat-Zinn notes, "Your life is already doing itself"—you just have to be mindful of it.[1] At some point and time in your recovery, you will wake up and you will realize that you have changed, and that that change feels natural—it feels like the real you. That is the day you'll know that you have hit your stride—that you have all the pieces you need to continue on, even on bad days. It's also the day that you'll truly realize that this recovery road has no endpoint; it's the road you're going to be walking for the rest of your life. So it's your job to make that walk a good one.

A while ago, I read this article in *National Geographic* that stuck with me over time. Something about it connected with me, and now I think I know why. It's about the arctic tern, a little bird with grey feathers and white markings, and a black top hat. She's a tiny thing but has an amazing amount of endurance. She makes the world's longest migration every year; her journey is a zigzagging 44,000 miles.

During her flight, she will choose routes that follow wind patterns that move her slowly forward so that she doesn't waste her energy flying directly into the wind. She also stops, rests, and refuels on the ocean from time to time to get her strength back. Her flight is all about strategies to help her traverse the distance every year. By the time her thirty-year life is over, the arctic tern will have flown around 1.5 million miles.[2]

You are seemingly fragile but capable of remarkable things. The tern never doubts that she will make it from her starting place to her ending place, and neither should you. Remember: hope is the thing with wings.

BE INSPIRED

One thing that has helped me on my path is the wisdom and inspiration of others. Over time, I've collected quotes and lines from poems and songs that have sparked a connection for me or created a new meaning for me, or made me feel less alone.

I screenshot this collection on my phone. I have friends that create meme boards that they post to Facebook and Pinterest, and other friends who write the things that inspire them on sticky notes and then post them around their house and office.

Collected inspiration and wisdom helped bolster me on my journey; perhaps they will for you too. You know that saying, "It takes a village"? Well, recovery takes a village and then some. Reach out. Talk. Listen. Learn. Share. See how it feels to walk this new road together instead of alone. Right now alone might feel familiar and comfortable, but get out there and live!

AUTOBIOGRAPHY IN FIVE SHORT CHAPTERS

Chapter One

I walk down the street.
> There is a deep hole in the sidewalk.
> I fall in.
> I am lost. . . . I am helpless.
>> It isn't my fault.
It takes forever to find a way out.

Chapter Two

I walk down the same street.
> There is a deep hole in the sidewalk.
> I pretend I don't see it.
> I fall in again.
I can't believe I am in this same place.
>> But, it isn't my fault.
It still takes a long time to get out.

Chapter Three

I walk down the same street.
> There is a deep hole in the sidewalk.
> I see it is there.
> I still fall in . . . it's a habit . . . but,
>> my eyes are open.
>> I know where I am.

It is *my* fault.
I get out immediately.

Chapter Four

I walk down the same street.
> There is a deep hole in the sidewalk.
> I walk around it.

Chapter Five

I walk down another street.

—Portia Nelson, *There's a Hole in My Sidewalk*

A Note about Relapse

The world can be a super harsh place, and people are people—fallible and fragile. This book is a guide to loving yourself and loving people, no matter what your history—your story—tells you about vulnerability. This is the great gift of being human: the awareness that things are unpredictable, like monsoonal moisture promising a lovely thunderstorm, and yet you awaken to a sunny day.

When my mom died this year, I thought a lot about how I reacted when my dad died in 2001. What a difference recovery makes. When my dad died, it was like I was incapable of weathering the storm of loss, of the uncertain path his death created in my heart. I really thought I would find the deepest sense of freedom from him being gone. I had built a lovely gilded birdcage of denial, and I lived there. The caged bird does sing; it sings a song of longing—a song of wishing for a better past. I mourned, I keened, I ultimately relapsed after he died.

The wires of love and devastation were crossed—so much so that I was unsure I would survive, but I did. I told my truth and I lived. And now I don't just live, I thrive. You can too.

After my mom died, I experienced such a different kind of mourning than I did with my dad. Mourning for my mom was sweet; it still is sweet. My mom loved so powerfully and with so little expectation of devotion that devotion came naturally. I miss her every day. I talk to her every night. I look for signs that she is still with me, and they come. I feel her presence in the way the light hits a particular photo of she and I that sits in a place of pride. I feel her in the sweet dreams I can recall as I slide into wakefulness in the early morning. And when I wear her black blazer or her sapphire ring, I feel the deepest love and gratitude. My mom died eighteen years sober, and she was a hardcore alcoholic for many years. I honor her and all of us by maintaining my own recovery.

Maintaining my own recovery has been, historically, not my strong suit. Relapse is real, and I did it chronically for a long time. In my earlier recovery, as I was living and loving my way to the ten-year mark, I felt untouchable, invincible, even complacent. But catastrophe doesn't announce its imminent arrival. There is no early warning system like for a tornado or an earthquake. People die and things fall apart, often without any advance notice. There are internal signs that, had I been mindfully checking in on myself, would have informed me that were things to fall apart, I would not be prepared to withstand the tempest. Now I have embraced mindfulness practices that allow me to be my own alert system; and in asking my clients to do the same, it keeps me on my toes. If I'm going to sit in a counseling session with someone and ask them to do these things but I am unwilling to do them as well, what does that say about my own ability and willingness to change?

But change I did, and I continue to be open to change. I don't always like it, but I remain open to it anyway. I want to live free and clear—open and willing. Ready to love and to receive love. If I'm loaded, I lose it all. . . .

—*LMP, September 30, 2016*

Acknowledgments

This book comes from my heart; and my heart has been profoundly affected by so many amazing people, I can only hope to acknowledge you all (which I won't, 'cause, you know, there's a whole lot of you!).

My beautiful mother, Suzy January. Thank you for showing me such love, such grace, and for helping me to see that I'd been identifying with the wrong parent for so long. I am my mother's daughter.

Shane, my loving and brilliant son. You teach me so much and show me new ways to consider old ideas. I thank you for loving me, and I love you to the moon and back.

My wonderful ex-husband, Shane Fontayne, and his incredible wife, Maria. We are a loving family, and the two of you are so dear to me.

My dearest Owen, Susan, Marissa, and Connie. My girls. Need I say more?

My Breathe Life Healing Centers family: you've all taught me so much, and it's an honor and a blessing to work with you guys. Kathleen Murphy, Deb Hughes, Brad Lamm, Leslie Crowley, Larry Hymes, Andrew Saunders, Donna Trujillo, Cara Westover, Miguel Palacios, David Hickman, Brandon Kneefel. Go Team Breathe! I love you all!

My sponsor Cindy, with whom I share so much, including the love of pugs.

Glenn Scarpelli and Jerry Gilden, this book would not be were it not for you two. My deep love and gratitude.

Everyone at Beyond Words for helping this project find its way. Thank you.

To all of my brothers and sisters in recovery, and to those striving to recover, there is a solution.

To all who've died of this terrible disease, I honor you by carrying the message, fighting the stigma, and reaching out my hand to the next one who hopes.

Richard Cohn and Michele Cohn, thank you, thank you, thank you!

Dear Anna Noak, thank you.

Nevin Mays, I thank you for helping to make a difficult transition ultimately seamless.

To all of my colleagues in the field of behavioral health, you are brave and giving warriors, and it's an honor to walk with you.

Last but certainly not least, Rudy, Franklin, One Eye, Louie, Mimi, Rama, Mohlee, Baby Cat, and Bubbles. Our little creature people, I love you all. You make my day, every day.

Notes

Introduction

1. "President Obama Proposes $1.1 Billion in New Funding to Address the Prescription Opioid Abuse and Heroin Use Epidemic," press release, The White House, Office of the Press Secretary, February 2, 2016, www.whitehouse.gov/the-press-office/2016/02/02/president-obama-proposes-11-billion-new-funding-address-prescription.

2. "Alcohol Facts and Statistics," National Institutes of Health website, last modified June 2016, pubs.niaaa.nih.gov/publications/AlcoholFacts&Stats/AlcoholFacts&Stats.htm.
3. Ibid.
4. Ibid.

Chapter 1

1. Russell Brand, *My Booky Wook: A Memoir of Sex, Drugs, and Stand-Up* (New York: It Books, 2010), 66.

2. National Institute on Drug Abuse, "The Science of Drug Abuse and Addiction: The Basics," National Institute on Drug Abuse website, last modified September 2014, www.drugabuse.gov /publications/media-guide/science-drug-abuse-addiction-basics.

3. National Institute on Drug Abuse, "Drugs, Brains, and Behavior: The Science of Addiction," National Institute on Drug Abuse website, last modified July 2014, www.drugabuse.gov/publications /drugs-brains-behavior-science-addiction/drug-abuse-addiction.

4. American Psychiatric Association, ed., *Diagnostic and Statistical Manual of Mental Disorders*, 5th ed. (Arlington, VA: American Psychiatric Association, 2013).

Chapter 2

1. don Miguel Ruiz, *The Four Agreements: A Practical Guide to Personal Freedom (A Toltec Wisdom Book)* (San Rafael, CA: Amber-Allen Publishing, 1997), 7–9.

2. Alcoholics Anonymous, *Alcoholics Anonymous: The Story of How Many Thousands of Men and Women Have Recovered from Alcoholism*, 4th ed. (New York: Alcoholics Anonymous World Services, Inc., 2002), 417.

3. Russell Brand, "The Only Way to Help Addicts Is to Treat Them Not as Bad People but as Sick People," *The Spectator*, March 9, 2013, www.spectator.co.uk/2013/03/fixing-a-hole/.

Chapter 4

1. Mark 9:24 (New American Standard Bible).

2. Sidney D. Piburn, *The Dalai Lama: A Policy of Kindness* (Delhi: Motilal Banarsidass, 2002), 38.

3. *Stanford Encyclopedia of Philosophy*, s.v. "Søren Kierkegaard," last modified July 8, 2016, plato.stanford.edu/entries/kierk egaard/#Reli.

4. Ibid.

Chapter 5

1. Chief Joseph, "Chief Joseph Surrenders" (in his surrender to the US Army, October 5, 1877), The History Place: Great Speeches Collection, accessed March 12, 2016, http://www.historyplace. com/speeches/joseph.htm.

2. Fred R. Shapiro, "Who Wrote the Serenity Prayer?" *The Chronicle Review*, The Chronicle of Higher Education website, April 28, 2014, chronicle.com/article/Who-Wrote-the-Serenity-Prayer -/146159/.

Chapter 7

1. Carlo C. DiClemente and J. O. Prochaska, "Toward a Comprehensive Model of Change: Stages of Change and Addictive Behaviors," *Treating Addictive Behaviors* (New York: Plenum Press, 1998), 3–24.

Chapter 8

1. "Shame about Past Alcoholism Predicts Relapse and Declining Health in Recovering Alcoholics," Association for Psychological Science website, February 4, 2013, www.psychologicalscience.org /index.php/news/releases/shame-about-past-alcoholism -predicts-relapse-and-declining-health-in-recovering-alcoholics .html.

Chapter 10

1. *Your Dictionary*, s.v. "grace," accessed March 12, 2016, http:// www.yourdictionary.com.

2. "Dealing with Fear in Recovery," AlcoholRehab.com, accessed March 12, 2016, alcoholrehab.com/addiction-recovery/dealing -with-fear-in-recovery/; David Sack, MD, "6 Common Fears in Addiction Recovery—and How to Face Them," *Addiction Recovery* (blog), Psych Central website, accessed March 12, 2016, blogs.psychcentral.com/addiction-recovery/2014/06/6-common -fears-in-addiction-recovery-and-how-to-face-them/.

Chapter 11

1. US Department of Health and Human Services, Administration for Children and Families, Administration on Children, Youth, and Families, Children's Bureau, *Child Maltreatment 2013*, (Washington, DC: Government Printing Office, 2015), x, https://www.acf.hhs.gov/sites/default/files/cb/cm2013.pdf.

2. Ibid., 43.

3. Khoury, Lamya, et al., "Substance Use, Childhood Traumatic Experience, and Posttraumatic Stress Disorder in an Urban Civilian Population," *Depression and Anxiety* 27, no. 12 (2010): 1077–1086, doi: 10.1002/da.20751.

4. *Wikipedia*, s.v. "Eye movement desensitization and reprocessing," last modified September 10, 2016, en.wikipedia.org/w/index.php?title=Eye_movement_desensitization_and_reprocessing&oldid=722796355.

Conclusion

1. Jon Kabat-Zinn, *Full Catastrophe Living: Using the Wisdom of Your Body and Mind to Face Stress, Pain, and Illness* (New York: Bantam, 2013), 580.

2. Mason Inman, "World's Longest Migration Found—2X Longer Than Thought," National Geographic News, National Geographic website, January 2, 2010, news.nationalgeographic.com/news/2010/01/100111-worlds-longest-migration-arctic-tern-bird/.

Resources

Government Resources

CDC—Centers for Disease Control and Prevention: A federal agency that tracks, detects, and investigates health issues. It also conducts research to promote healthy behaviors and prevent diseases. www.cdc.gov

NIAAA—National Institute on Alcohol Abuse and Alcoholism: Under the National Institutes of Health, NIAAA conducts and supports research in the effort to reduce alcohol-related problems. www.niaaa.nih.gov

NIDA—National Institute on Drug Abuse: An institute that researches drug abuse and addiction to improve prevention, treatment, and policy. www.drugabuse.gov

NREPP—National Registry of Evidence-Based Programs and Practices: A searchable online registry of mental health and substance abuse interventions, provided by the Substance Abuse and Mental Health Services Administration (SAMHSA). www.samhsa .gov/nrepp

SAMHSA—Substance Abuse and Mental Health Services Administration: A branch of the US Department of Health and Human services, SAMHSA is charged with improving the quality and availability of prevention, treatment, and rehabilitative services to address substance abuse and mental illness. www.samhsa.gov

Public Education Resources

The Anonymous People is a feature documentary film about the more than 23 million Americans living in long-term recovery from addiction to alcohol and other drugs. www.manuyfaces1voice.org

Easy-to-Read Drug Facts offers plain-language drug facts, audio, and videos from the National Institute on Drug Abuse. www.easy read.drugabuse.gov

The Hungry Heart is an intimate look at the often hidden world of prescription drug addiction. www.kingdomcountry.org/product /hungry-heart/

Shatterproof is a new national organization committed to protecting our children from addiction to alcohol and other drugs, and ending the stigma and suffering of those affected by this disease. www.shatterproof.org

Warning: Take Only as Directed is a free, short musical film and curriculum based on a personal tragedy that will serve to reduce teen prescription drug abuse. Available to download on the film's website: www.warningshortfilm.com.

Treatment and Recovery Resources

AddictionCenter.com is a resource for connecting those with addictions and their loved ones to the help they need to put their lives back together. www.addictioncenter.com

Alcoholics Anonymous is an international movement to provide treatment for alcoholics using a 12-step program and group meetings. www.aa.org

Behavioral Health Treatment Services Locator is a service provided by SAMHSA that helps you find the best alcohol and drug treatment programs using a large database of qualified recovery centers. www.findtreatment.samhsa.gov

Helping Others Live Sober offers resources for professionals in the addiction medicine field as well as for those in recovery. This service is provided by the Case Western Reserve University School of Medicine, Department of Psychiatry, and Division of Child Psychiatry. www.helpingotherslivesober.org

National Institute on Drug Abuse has a resource called "Seeking Drug Abuse Treatment: Know What to Ask," which offers five important questions to ask when looking for an effective treatment program. www.drugabuse.gov/publications/seeking-drug-abuse-treatment-know-what-to-ask/introduction

The Support Group Project is an online directory to help families across the country find the support they need in the face of a loved one's addiction. www.supportgroupproject.org

Recommended Reading

The Big Book by Bill W.

The Big Book (its technical name is *Alcoholics Anonymous: The Story of How Many Thousands of Men and Women Have Recovered from Alcoholism*) was published in 1939 and is where the 12-step program comes from. A great deal of what the general public understands about addiction comes from this book. Things such as "finding a greater power," "once an alcoholic, always an alcoholic," and "recovery happens one day at a time" are all ideas expressed in the book.

The Big Book is full of some really great stuff, but not all of it is for everyone (especially the God / higher power stuff). I do recommend you read the first 164 pages of the book. If you can identify yourself in those pages, then this book will help you acknowledge the crappy fact that you're an addict.

I once had a client in his early twenties who would loudly and often declare his hate for 12-step recovery. I believe his sentiment was something along the lines of "Fuck this!" Even so, I gave him a copy of the Big Book and told him to just give it a shot and read it. I was pretty sure that he was going to chuck it in the trash the minute I walked away.

About a week later, I saw him, and to my great surprise, he was sitting there on the couch reading the Big Book. I stopped and exclaimed, "Dude!" He said, "I'm so pissed at you." When I asked him why, he declared, "This is me," pointing at the book. "These guys in 1939 are describing me, and I'm not even an alcoholic. I'm a heroine addict, and this is me. I'm identifying myself on every page of this book."

Hey, knowing is half the battle.

The Body Keeps the Score by Bessel van der Kolk, MD

The Body Keeps the Score: Brain, Mind, and Body in the Healing of Trauma was published in 2014 and is a guide through how traumatic experiences can overwhelm and mess with the development of the brain, mind, and body. The book is a mix of scientific research and real stories about people who have experienced trauma. All of it combines together to lead you to a place where you can both understand how trauma impacts your life and start healing from it.

I found *The Body Keeps the Score* to be really helpful in connecting all of the dots. A little more technical than the other books on my list, it is still full of a lot of aha moments, particularly if you're a survivor of any kind of abuse or trauma.

Emotional Sobriety by Tian Dayton

Emotional Sobriety: From Relationship Trauma to Resilience and Balance was published in 2007, and is a holistic approach to managing unhealthy coping mechanisms and behaviors. It's another connect-the-dots kind of book that is compassionate and full of great wisdom.

The first time I read it, I saw myself on every page; and on every page, I found something that gave me hope.

The Four Agreements by don Miguel Ruiz

The Four Agreements: A Practical Guide to Personal Freedom (A Toltec Wisdom Book) was published in 1997. It is a book that promotes personal freedom from limiting beliefs and agreements that create unhappiness in our lives.

When I first read this book, it was like an epiphany. The best metaphor I have for it is that I realized I was operating from Windows 7 when in fact there's a whole new operating system. It was crazy to realize that all these things that were domesticated into me through trauma, abuse, and neglect—things that I brought into my adult life— were no longer useful or true.

Indie Spiritualist by Chris Grosso

Chris Grosso is an example of what it really means to examine your choices and your life, and to ultimately accept yourself, your imperfections, and your humanity. His book, *Indie Spiritualist: A No Bullshit Exploration of Spirituality*, is a raw and honest look into his path toward and through recovery. He shows you how to be both spiritual and individual. You can walk your own path even when you're navigating by the cairns stacked by those who came before you. If you're not sure about all the spiritual stuff, Grosso's book might help you figure that out.

The Mastery of Love by don Miguel Ruiz

The Mastery of Love: A Practical Guide to the Art of Relationship (A Toltec Wisdom Book) was published in 1999, and it illuminates the fear-based beliefs and assumptions that undermine love, leading to suffering and drama in our relationships. It is full of stories that show us how to heal our wounds.

I gobbled this book up. Nearly every page had new wisdom. The biggest thing it taught me was what I am and am not responsible for in a relationship. Out of that, the biggest aha was realizing that I'm not responsible for other people's happiness. It helped me understand that people in pain cause pain for other people, and it gave me things that I can do to manage the complexity of it all.

Scar Tissue by Anthony Kiedis of the Red Hot Chili Peppers and *Heroin Diaries* by Nikky Sixx of Mötley Crüe

Scar Tissue and *Heroin Diaries: A Year in the Life of a Shattered Rock Star* were published in 2005 and 2008 respectively, and are autobiographic books written by two hardcore rockers with substance use disorder. I recommend both of these because, first, they let you know that you aren't alone and, second, they are books by people who are self-aware, which can help others become self-aware through example.

Reading these books is just another way to see how bad it can get and how good it can get. There's a little bit of voyeurism in reading these serious books about serious addiction. There's also a sort of out-of-body experience thing that happens as you're reading from a sober point of view about someone who's shooting coke in the closet. It takes you a moment, and then you think, *Hey, I used to do that!*

Raw, honest, dark, humorous, and starkly human, both of these books are also just plain, old, good reads.

There's a Hole in My Sidewalk by Portia Nelson

There's a Hole in My Sidewalk is a little book with a big message on personal responsibility. It takes the reader from denial, to recognition, to acceptance, and to a new unfolding future. The lead poem, "Autobiography in Five Short Chapters," is used by many 12-step programs. Portia's words resonate at a heart level, providing insight and inspiration as we each find our way on the path to self-discovery.

This list is obviously not an exhaustive one, so get more recommen-
dations from your counselor, trusted friends, and family members;
from trusted websites and blogs; and from your own exploration.
Not all of the books you read need to be or should be about recovery.
A good book can, by its very nature, give us a bit of respite and even
grace for as long as we are in its pages.

Three grand essentials to happiness in this life
are something to do, something to love,
and something to hope for.

—Joseph Addison

Mackenzie Phillips is an actress and singer best known for her roles in *American Graffiti* and as rebellious teenager Julie Cooper on the sitcom *One Day at a Time*. She is most recently known for her role on Disney channel's science-fiction show *So Weird*. Mackenzie is the daughter of John Phillips, lead singer of the '60s band The Mamas and the Papas. As a troubled teen star, Phillips made several visits to rehab before getting sober. Her struggles with addiction have been well documented in her bestselling memoir *High on Arrival* and in the media. She now wishes to use her past experiences to help others and offer hope to individuals who are struggling with substance abuse and addiction.